ZONDERVAN
Charts

CHARTS OF

CHRISTIAN ETHICS

Books in the Zondervan*Charts* Series

Charts of Ancient and Medieval Church History (John D. Hannah)

Charts of Bible Prophecy (H. Wayne House and Randall Price)

Charts of Christian Theology and Doctrine (H. Wayne House)

Charts of Christian Ethics (Craig Vincent Mitchell)

Charts of Church History (H. Wayne House)

Charts of Cults, Sects, and Religious Movements (H. Wayne House)

Charts of the Gospels and the Life of Christ (Robert L. Thomas)

Charts of Modern and Postmodern Church History (John D. Hannah)

Charts of World Religions (H. Wayne House)

Chronological and Background Charts of Church History (Robert C. Walton)

Chronological and Background Charts of the New Testament (H. Wayne House)

Chronological and Background Charts of the Old Testament (John H. Walton)

Chronological and Thematic Charts of Philosophies and Philosophers (Milton D. Hunnex)

Taxonomic Charts of Theology and Biblical Studies (M. James Sawyer)

Timeline Charts of the Western Church (Susan Lynn Peterson)

ZONDERVAN

CHARTS OF

CHRISTIAN ETHICS

OVER 100 CHARTS

Craig Vincent Mitchell

ZONDERVAN™

GRAND RAPIDS, MICHIGAN 49530 USA

ZONDERVAN.COM/
AUTHORTRACKER

We want to hear from you. Please send your comments about this
book to us in care of zreview@zondervan.com. Thank you.

ZONDERVAN

Charts of Christian Ethics
Copyright © 2006 by Craig Vincent Mitchell

Requests for information should be addressed to:

Zondervan, *Grand Rapids, Michigan 49530*

Library of Congress Cataloging-in-Publication Data

Mitchell, Craig Vincent
    Charts of Christian ethics / Craig Vincent Mitchell.
       p. cm.—(ZondervanCharts)
    ISBN 978-0-310-25452-2
    1. Christian ethics—Charts, diagrams, etc. I. Title. II. Series.
    BJ1261.M58 2005
    241'.022'3—dc22

2005017159

Interior design by Angela Moulter

Printed in the United States of America

Dedicated to my grandmothers:
Ethel Roberts and Sue Mitchell

I thank the Lord for these women who were always
models of Christian virtue. They taught me how
to trust in the Lord and follow after him.
I thank the Lord for their example
and their prayers for me.

Contents

Part 3: Biblical Foundations of Christian Ethics

Part 4: Theological Foundations of Christian Ethics

God

Creation

Man

Church

State and Church

Part 5: History of Ethics

Historical Overview

The Premodern Era

The Modern Era

Postmodern Era

PHILOSOPHICAL FOUNDATIONS OF ETHICS

The Elements of Philosophy

Philosophy

Philosophy is the investigation of the nature, causes, or principles of

1. reality

2. knowledge and/or

3. values based on

4. logical reasoning rather than empirical methods

Logic	**Logic** underlies the study of the three branches of philosophy. It is the study of the principles of reasoning (especially of the *structure* of propositions as distinguished from their *content*) and of method and validity in deductive reasoning (from Gk. *logikos*, "reasoning," derived from *logos*, "word" or "reason"). (→2)

Reality	**Metaphysics** is the branch of philosophy that examines the nature of reality (from Gk. *meta + physika*, literally "after physics," the title of Aristotle's treatise on first principles that followed his work on physics). (→3–6)

Knowledge	**Epistemology** (from Gk. *epistēmē*, "knowledge") is the branch of philosophy that studies the nature of knowledge. (→7–10)

Values	**Axiology** is the branch of philosophy that deals with the nature of values and value judgments (from Gk. *axios*, "worth"). (→11–14)

Chart 1

Logic

Logic

DEDUCTIVE LOGIC *Uses one or more premises and a conclusion (together called a* **syllogism***). If the premises are true, then the conclusion will be true as well. Consequently, deductive logic can provide a high level of certainty.*	**Symbolic Logic**	Also known as **formal logic**. It includes a number of modern and traditional approaches to logic.	
	Mathematics	The study of quantities, magnitudes, and forms, generally with the use of numbers and symbols.	
	Modal Logic *A branch of logic that deals not with the truth or falsity of propositions, but with their* **modalities***, that is, properties of propositions, such as necessity, contingency, possibility, and impossibility. Thus it deals not with metaphysical necessities, but with the manner in which things manifest themselves. "Some men may be immortal" is a modal proposition.*	**Epistemic Logic**	A kind of modal logic employed to ascertain what one should know in all possible worlds.
		Deontic Logic	A kind of modal logic employed to ascertain what one ought to do in all possible worlds. Necessity is replaced with ought.
INDUCTIVE LOGIC *Tied to probability. For example, it is a safe bet that the sun will rise tomorrow. Inductive logic cannot provide certainty because it depends on probability.*	**Abduction**	An approach to logic developed by Charles Sanders Peirce (1839–1914) to explain a set of data. This is also known as **inference to the best explanation**.	
	Logic of Explanation	Attempts to understand how or why something is the way it is. This involves an examination of the possible causes for a given state of affairs.	
	Probability Theory	A judgment based on the mathematical likelihood of a given event.	

Chart 2

Metaphysics

Metaphysics

The three branches of metaphysics

Ontology	Ontology is concerned with existence, or being; it can also include such things as free will/determinism, substance, and immortality of the soul. The term *ontology* is often equated with *metaphysics.*
Cosmology	Cosmology is concerned with time, space, and causation.
Theology	Theology is concerned with the nature and existence of God and his relationship to all of reality.

In metaphysics, a number of common words are used in a specialized sense:

proposition	A **proposition** is a statement about reality that is true or false.
fact	A **fact** is something in reality that makes a proposition true.
event	An **event** is a proposition about a specific time and place.
state of affairs	A **state of affairs** is a statement about reality that may either obtain or fail to obtain.
world	A **world** is a situation in which a proposition and its opposite cannot exist at the same time and place.
book	A **book** is a set of propositions that describes a world.
necessary	For something to be **necessary** means that it must exist in any possible world.
contingent	Something that is **contingent** is dependent on something that is necessary for its existence. Something that is contingent can fail to exist in any possible world.
teleology	**Teleology** teaches that the world has a purpose and is in process to fulfill it.

Chart 3

Ontology

Property and Substance *Concerned with how things exist.*	**Realism** suggests that there are universals and particulars. Realism also suggests that things exist independent of the observer. Thus realism can be viewed as materialism and idealism in interaction. (Materialism assumes that matter/energy or the space-time continuum are all that exist.)	
	Nominalism suggests that only particulars exist. Thus nominalism denies that there are such things as real essences.	
	Idealism assumes that the world and the objects in it are dependent on the mind for their existence.	**Subjective idealism** suggests that what we experience or perceive is nothing more than ideas (George Berkeley). **Objective idealism** suggests that the material world is just a shadow of the real world. The real world is the world of the forms (Plato).
Mind/Body Problem *Attempts to resolve the problems associated with the interaction between the mind and the body.*	**Interactionism**—Mind and body do interact.	
	Occasionalism—Mind and body do not interact. They are synchronized by God.	
	Materialism—There are only brain processes. There are no mental events.	
	Idealism—There are no physical events. Everything is a mental/spiritual picture. Reality is an illusion.	
	Panentheism—Physical and mental events are the same, because God is *in* everything (not God *is* everything, which is pantheism).	
Free Will and Determinism *Examines the degree to which one is responsible for one's actions and the external forces involved in these actions.*	**Free Will**—One is ultimately free to do as one chooses, uninfluenced by external constraints.	
	Compatibilism—This position attempts to reconcile free will with determinism.	
	Determinism—This is the idea that external forces act upon something in such a way that there is no free will.	
Personal Identity *Concerned with the nature and existence of the self.*	**Self**—What is the nature of the self?	
	Identity through Time—How do change and time affect the self?	
	Life after Death—Does the self continue after death?	

Chart 4

Cosmology

Time *The temporal aspect of reality.*	**Perceptual Time**—Time as it appears to an observer.
	Conceptual Time—Time as it actually is. • **A Theory**—A tenseless view of time. The only aspect of time that exists is the present. The past exists only as memory. It rejects the idea of a space-time continuum. • **B Theory**—A view that all three tenses of time exist simultaneously. It accepts the idea of the space-time continuum.
Space *The spatial aspect of reality.*	**Perceptual Space**—Space as it is perceived by an observer.
	Conceptual Space—Space as it actually is.
Causation *What relates one event in reality temporally to another event.*	**First Cause**—The cause of all other causes.
	Formal Cause—The shape or "blueprint" to which an entity conforms.
	Material Cause—The physical "stuff" of which something is made.
	Efficient Cause—Forces or activities/agents that produce an entity.
	Final Cause—The purpose for which an entity exists.

Space-Time Continuum—An idea explained in Einstein's special theory of revelation. It asserts that space and time are interlinked as aspects of a four-dimensional universe. There are three spatial dimensions and one temporal dimension.

The Aristotelian Chain of Causes

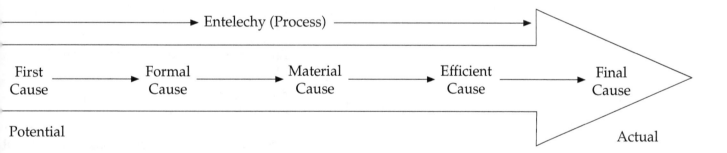

Chart 5

Theology/Philosophy of Religion

GOD'S NATURE	**Number of Gods**	**Monotheism**—There is only one god. **Polytheism**—There is a multitude of gods.	
	God's Attributes	Necessity, power, knowledge, presence, goodness, etc.	
	God's Relation to Creation	**Transcendence**—God is beyond the ordinary world of human experience. **Immanence**—God remains close to and intimately involved with creation. **Panentheism**—A special case of immanence that posits God is *in* everything. **Pantheism**—God *is* everything.	
RELIGIOUS EPISTEMOLOGY *(See also chart 7, "Epistemology.")*	**Hermeneutics**	**Trust**	A belief that the Bible can be trusted as a legitimate source of knowledge.
		Doubt	A belief that human reason must be trusted over the Bible. It suggests that a scientific approach must be taken to biblical interpretation.
		Suspicion	A belief that the writers of the Bible are merely attempting to force their values on the reader. This position argues that the author is dead and that meaning is determined by the reader or the community that he or she is part of.
	Apologetics	**Classical**	Employs logical arguments to defend God's existence.
		Evidential	Employs the facts of history to defend belief in God.
		Cumulative	Employs all apologetic methods together to defend belief in God.
		Presuppositional	Asserts that the presuppositions of the biblical worldview are the only ones that people can live with consistently. It emphasizes the preaching of the gospel.

Chart 6

Theories of Truth

All theories of truth have a metaphysical component and an epistemological component. The metaphysical component is concerned with the object of truth. All theories of knowledge involve true belief.

Theory	Metaphysics	Epistemology	Explanation
Correspondence theory of truth	Metaphysical realism. Metaphysics is first philosophy in this theory.	Knowledge corresponds to reality.	Truth corresponds to reality. This theory requires objective reality and not opinion.
Coherence theory of truth	Metaphysical nominalism. In some cases involves metaphysical idealism.	Knowledge is based on reason or justification. Epistemology is first philosophy in this theory of truth.	Truth requires a coherent set of beliefs without contradictions. This approach to truth is objective, but does not require reality.
Pragmatic theory of truth	Metaphysical nominalism. In some cases involves metaphysical idealism.	Knowledge is based upon justification, which comes from sensory experience. Epistemology is first philosophy in this theory of truth.	Truth is what works. This approach involves a subjective view of truth.
Semantic (Tarski's theory of truth)	Metaphysical nominalism	Knowledge is an empirical-inductive (scientific) activity.	This approach to truth was developed by analytic philosophers. It requires objective reality. Philosophy of language is first philosophy for this theory of truth.

Chart 7

Epistemology

Epistemology

THEORIES OF KNOWLEDGE	**Internalism** • Knowledge is justified true belief. • The knower must know *how* he or she knows. • Skepticism is a significant problem. • Deontological approach to knowledge.	**Foundationalism** • Suggests that knowledge is a structure in which one piece of knowledge rests upon another. • Foundation of this structure of knowledge must be properly basic. • Is compatible with the correspondence and coherence theories of truth (see below). **Coherentism** • Suggests that knowledge is a structure in which each piece of knowledge depends on every other. • Compatible with correspondence and coherence theories of truth (see below). • Is actually another form of foundationalism.
	Externalism • Requires correspondance theory of truth or semantic theory of truth. • Knowledge is true belief produced by a reliable belief-forming process. • Does not require the knower to know how he or she knows. • Teleological approach to knowledge.	**Naturalized Epistemology** • Knowledge results from natural processes. Reduces epistemology to cognitive science. **Virtue Epistemology** • Knowledge results from sensory experience, memory, and reason (both inductive and deductive). The intellectual virtues regulate belief-forming. **Functionalism Proper** • Knowledge results from the sensory and intellectual faculties operating in the way they are designed to in the proper environment.
SOURCES OF KNOWLEDGE	**Rationalism**	Knowledge results primarily from **reason**.
	Empiricism	Knowledge results primarily from **sensory experience**.

Chart 8

David Hume (1711–76)

Kinds of Knowledge	Analytic	Synthetic
A Priori *A priori knowledge does not depend on sensory experience but results from deduction.*	• Necessary truths. • Tautologies. • Definitions. • Mathematics. • Cannot possibly be false. *Hume believed that all analytic truths are a priori and vice versa. He also thought that these truths are trivial.*	
A Posteriori *A posteriori knowledge is knowledge based on sensory experience.*		• Empirical truths. • Not true by definition. • Matters of fact. *Hume thought that all synthetic truths are a posteriori and vice versa. All significant knowledge results only from sensory experience.*

Hume's **fork**	All knowledge is either a *necessary* truth or an *empirical* truth. All else is nonsense that must be rejected.
Hume's **argument against causation**	1. We can know that one thing follows another, but we cannot know that one thing causes another. 2. Knowledge of causes and effects is the result of sensory experience and not reason. 3. Thus we cannot know that everything has a cause.
Hume's **argument against induction**	Induction is based on probability or past occurrences. Just because things have always worked in a certain way before does not mean that they will continue to do so.
Hume's **conclusion**	We can actually know very little.

Chart 9

Immanuel Kant (1724–1804)

Kinds of Knowledge	Analytic	Synthetic
A Priori *A priori knowledge does not depend on sensory experience but results from deduction.*	• Tautologies (self-referential statements, e.g., "All bachelors are men"). • Definitions. *Kant held that all analytic truths are a priori but, contrary to Hume, not vice versa.*	• Mathematics. • Logic. • God's existence. *This is Kant's special category of knowledge.*
A Posteriori *A posteriori knowledge is knowledge based on sensory experience.*		• Sensory experience. *All a posteriori truths are synthetic but not vice versa.*

Kant's Transcendental Analysis of Mental Faculties

Mental Faculty	Synthetic A Priori
Perception *or intuition*	• Space. • Time. • Causation.
Understanding *Enables people to understand facts about the world.*	• Categories of understanding. • Mathematics.
Reason	• God. • The soul. • Freedom. • Morality.

The World according to Kant

Phenomenal World	Noumenal World
The realm of sensory experience. According to Kant, one can know only what is in the phenomenal world.	The world as it actually is. Kant believed that one cannot really know what is in the noumenal world.

Chart 10

Axiology

Value Theory

The primary questions in value theory:
(1) Is value a property of objects? (2) Is value objective or subjective?

Definition of Value	**Value**	A benefit-oriented motivation for action. Values are ideals that have to do with the vision people have of the good life for themselves and their communities. Values function both as constraints and as stimuli for action.
	Disvalue	A motivation for action that is not benefit oriented.
	Intrinsic Value	What something is valued as, as "an end" or "for itself." The ultimate end value of a thing.
	Instrumental Value	What is valued for the sake of something else. A value that is a "means" to an end.
Terminology of Value	**Value Object**	The object that is being evaluated.
	Locus of Value	An objective reason for value, e.g., "Education is of great value for living the good life."
	Underlying Value	Unstated values that are still important factors in decision making.
	Value Subscriber	A person who subscribes to a certain value or group of values.
	Evaluation	A judgment regarding a value object.
Value Experience	**Brentano/Meinong Value Theory**	Franz Brentano developed a theory of value that is based on emotion. All valuation can be described in terms of love or hate. Love and hate can have different levels or degrees. His student Alexius Meinong further developed Brentano's theory and explained what is necessary for any theory of value.
	Value Subject	The value subscriber who experiences.
	Emotion	A positive or negative emotion called the value feeling regarding the value object.
	Value Object	That which is being evaluated.
	Existence Judgment	A judgment about the realization or the existence of the value object.

Chart 11

Ethics

Metaethics	Metaphysics of Morals	Concerned with the nature of morality, more specifically, with the status of moral facts. Also concerned with freewill/determinism.
The foundations of morality	Moral Epistemology	Concerned with how one knows right and wrong.
	Moral Psychology	Concerned with the nature of the moral self.
Normative Ethics	Teleology	Concerned with the nature or purpose of a thing. Dependent on metaphysics.
	Deontology	Independent of metaphysics. Concerned only with rules or laws.
Ethical theory	Consequentialism	Concerned with the outcome of an act.
	Nonconsequentialism	Not concerned with the outcome of an act.

Chart 12

Aesthetics (1)

Meta-aesthetics *The foundations of beauty*	**Metaphysics of Beauty** *Concerned with the nature of beauty.*	**Realism**	Aesthetic facts exist independent of the observer.
		Irrealism	Aesthetic facts do not exist but are useful for appraising art.
		Nihilism	Aesthetic facts do not exist and are not even useful.
	Aesthetic Epistemology *Concerned with how one knows beauty.*	**Aesthetic Sense**	Aesthetic knowledge results from an aesthetic sense called taste (perhaps the passions).
		Reason	Aesthetic knowledge results from reason.
		Intuition	Aesthetic knowledge results via some unknown means (perhaps the passions).
	Aesthetic Psychology *Concerned with the aesthetic experience.*	**Aesthetic Experience**	What is the nature of the aesthetic experience and what causes it?
		Aesthetic Development	How does one develop the ability to appraise an aesthetic experience?
Aesthetic Theory	**Teleology**		Beauty depends on the nature of a thing. In other words, it depends on metaphysics.
	Deontology		Beauty depends on a set of objective rules.
Aesthetic Objects	**Natural Beauty**		Aesthetic experience resulting from natural objects.
	Art		Aesthetic experience resulting from man-made objects.

Chart 13

Aesthetics (2): Art

The Nature of Art	**Imitation**	Art is a secondhand copy of reality.
	Play	Art is an example of the creative process.
	Escape	Art is an escape from the real world.
	Expressionism	Art communicates feelings.
Expressionism	**Romanticism**	Art should communicate the artist's feelings.
	Object	The perceiver should recognize the emotion contained or reflected in the art object.
	Appraiser	Art should evoke feelings in the appraiser.
Subjectivism	**Cultural Relativism**	Aesthetic experience varies with culture.
	Postmodernism	Aesthetic experience is subjective and is determined by power.
Objectivism	**Absolutism**	Aesthetic experience is objective and should be the same for everyone.
	Educated Observer	Aesthetic experience is the result of education.

Chart 14

Philosophies

Major Movements in Analytic Philosophy

The "Linguistic Turn" is about the movement from epistemology to philosophy of language. Philosophy of language is considered first philosophy in the study of analytic philosophy. The other branches of philosophy are understood in light of the changes in philosophy of language. According to Quentin Smith (in *Ethical and Religious Thought in Analytic Philosophy of Language*), there are five major movements in analytic philosophy. Because intentionality is seen as a central feature of meaning, and intentionality is a feature of the mind, philosophy of language is merging with philosophy of the mind.

Logical Realism	**G. E. Moore** **Bertrand Russell**	The **Logical Realists (LR)** thought that language is essential to doing good philosophy. These philosophers are metaphysical realists who assert that every word in a sentence correlates to a sense or meaning.
Logical Positivism	**A. J. Ayer** **F. P. Ramsey** **Moritz Schlick** **Rudolf Carnap** **Otto Neurath**	Carnap defined philosophy as the analysis of the language of science. This language of science is concerned with both scientific uses and everyday life. A key idea is the verification principle which argues that anything that is not empirically verifiable is meaningless. They also emphasized the fact/value dichotomy.
Ordinary Language Analysis	**Ludwig Wittgenstein** **J. L. Austin** **Gilbert Ryle** **R. M. Hare** **P. F. Strawson** **John Searle**	Started by Ludwig Wittgenstein, ordinary language analysts reject the verification principle because they argue that it is senseless by its own standard. These philosophers argued that there are no metaphysical problems. There are, instead, only language problems. Philosophical statements are empirical generalizations about how ordinary expressions are used. These philosophers argue that the sense of an expression is its ordinary use.
Post-Positivists or Physicalists	**W. V. O. Quine** **Wilfrid Sellars** **D. M. Armstrong** **David Lewis** **Paul Churchland**	Started by Quine, this movement arose in response to both logical positivism and ordinary language analysis. These philosophers rejected the fact/value dichotomy. They held the belief that physical reality is the microscopic or macroscopic referents of the theoretical sentences in the physical sciences. As such, these philosophers have a place for metaphysics. In many cases, they attempt to reduce philosophy to hard sciences.
Linguistic Essentialism	**Saul Kripke** **Alvin Plantinga** **Robert Adams** **David Brink**	The **Logical Essentialists (LE)** agree with the post-positivists that metaphysics is a legitimate field of study. This movement resulted from the ideas of Saul Kripke expressed in his work *Naming and Necessity*. By employing the use of possible worlds and necessity, the essentialists consider what is essential to trans-world identities.

Chart 15

Philosophy of Language

The Nature of Language	**Grammar**	Concerned with the forms and structures of words. This includes the arrangement of words in sentences and phrases.
	Symbolic Systems	Examines the range of things that can be communicated through symbols of various sorts.
	Analyticity	Concerned with the priority of language over the mind (or vice versa).
	Theories of Meaning	Concerned with what meaning is and what it is related to.
Language and the Mind	**Innate Ideas**	Concerned with whether innate ideas provide a foundation for language and communication.
	Private Language	Concerned with the existence of language internal to the individual.
	Intentionality	Explores the relationship between communication and the intention of the communicator.
Language and Metaphysics	**The World**	Concerned with how language represents the world and our thoughts about the world.
	Truth	What is the relationship between language and truth?
Semiotics	**Semantics**	The branch of linguistics concerned with the nature, structure, and development of the meanings of signs and symbols. Focuses on epistemology as well as on semantic theories and mental states.
	Pragmatics	The study of language that focuses attention on the users and on the context of language use rather than on reference, truth, or grammar.
	Hermeneutics	The art and science of interpretation.
	Syntax	Concerned with the arrangement of words as elements in a sentence to show their relationship to one another.

Chart 16

Philosophy of Science

Science	An empirical, inductive approach to knowledge.
Scientific Method	Scientific realists believe there is a scientific method that uses the following hierarchy of concepts: • **Hypothesis**—An unproved theory, proposition, or supposition. • **Theory**—A hypothesis that has passed every objective test, thus yielding greater certainty that it is true. • **Law**—A theory that passes every conceivable test, thus yielding the highest level of certainty that can be achieved. Scientific antirealists do not believe that there is a scientific method.

Metaphysics of Science

Realism *Scientific theories accurately model reality.*	1. **Semantic realism** suggests that statements about theoretical entities are to be understood literally. 2. **Reductionism** suggests that theoretical entities are constructions out of more familiar materials.
Antirealism *Scientific theories cannot and do not model reality.*	**Instrumentalism** suggests that scientific theories are only useful but do not accurately model reality.

Epistemology of Science

Realism *One can know that a scientific theory is true.*	1. The best scientific theories are true. 2. The best scientific theories are close to the truth. 3. We are rationally justified to believe that the best scientific theories are true or close to the truth. 4. **Minimal epistemic realism** asserts that it is logically possible to attain a state that warrants belief in a theory.
Antirealism *One cannot know whether a scientific theory is true.*	**Constructive empiricism** suggests that science does not aim at truth. Instead, science only aims at empirical adequacy. In other words, it provides information that meets the scientist's purposes.

Reasons for Realism and Antirealism

Realism	**Success of Science**	Applied science demonstrates the realism of scientific theories.
Antirealism	**Theory of Underdetermination**	Theory underdetermines data. In other words, for any given set of data, there are an infinite number of theories that can account for it.
	Thomas Kuhn In *The Structure of Scientific Revolutions* Kuhn argues that scientists are not objective or fair. They operate out of self-interest by preserving the status quo. Younger scientists challenge the status quo through experimentation and demonstrate that the current paradigm is wrong. This results in a **paradigm shift.**	

Chart 17

Philosophy of Mind

The Mind-Body Problem	**Interactionism**	Physical events cause mental events, and mental events cause physical events.
	Occasionalism	Nicolas Malebranche (1638–1715) taught that mental events and physical events are synchronized by God. However, there is no interaction between the mind and body.
	Materialism	Only brain processes exist, because either there is no mind or mental events are epiphenomenal, i.e., secondary though related phenomena.
	Idealism	George Berkeley (1685–1753) asserted that there are no physical events. Everything (except the spiritual) exists only insofar as it is perceived through the senses.
	Pantheism	Baruch Spinoza (1632–77) asserted that mental and physical events are the same, because he believed that God is everything.
	Functionalism	Brain matter is not essential for brain functions. Computers with artificial intelligence can duplicate the function of the brain.
	Behaviorism	Mental events are only tendencies to behave in particular ways.
	Identity Theory	Mental events are identical to brain functions.
Personal Identity	**Personal Identity and Time**	Does the self change with time, or does one become another person?
	The Self	What is the nature of the self?
	Agency	What is the will, and how are decisions made?
Cognitive Science	**Cognition**	What is consciousness? How does it work?
	Emotion	What is the nature of the emotions, and how do they relate to cognition?
	Action	How do individual acts relate to cognition?

Chart 18

American Pragmatism

American pragmatism is a mixture of empiricism and idealism. It holds that a theory is to be accounted true as long as it works. Pragmatists believe that all experience is value laden. Much of American analytic philosophy was influenced by pragmatism. American analytic philosophers who subscribed to pragmatism include such figures as W. V. O. Quine, Hilary Putnam, and Richard Rorty. Some types of pragmatism (like Rorty's) lead to postmodernity.

Charles Sanders Peirce (1839–1914)	Peirce founded American pragmatism. The purpose of pragmatism is to make ideas clear. He coined the term *pragmaticism* to differentiate his views from those of William James. He subscribed to metaphysical realism and rejected Cartesian certainty and methodological doubt.
	Peirce saw three kinds of truth: • **Transcendental truth**—The real character of a thing. What science attempts to ascertain. • **Complex truth**—The truth of propositions. • **Logical truth**—The conformity of a proposition to reality. Experience can refute or affirm this kind of truth. Every proposition is either true or false.
	Pragmatic theory of meaning—The meaning of an idea is the sum of its practical consequences.
William James (1842–1910)	James was influenced by Peirce. He viewed pragmatism as radical empiricism. Pragmatism is only a method to settle metaphysical disputes. He used pragmatism as a type of therapy.
	Pragmatic theory of truth—Truth in our ideas means their ability to work. Truth is the "cash value" of an idea.
	Pragmatic theory of meaning—The practical outcome of a belief is its true meaning.
John Dewey (1859–1952)	Dewey described his position as **empirical naturalism** or **naturalistic empiricism**.
	Pragmatic instrumentalism—Knowledge is only for solving problems. This does not deny the objectivity of truth, because knowledge is not made relative to any individual.

Chart 19

Existentialism
(Existence precedes essence)

Definition	Existentialism is not a system because it is not based on an ontology that includes any type of essence; instead, it does philosophy from the phenomenological perspective, that is, the perspective from the point of view of the individual. It is rather a set of ideas that result from a modern emphasis on the individual. Existentialism teaches that existence precedes essence, meaning that it denies that objective truth has the priority in philosophical thought.	
Themes	**Free Will**	The rejection of determinism and fate.
	Choice	Each individual is free to choose how he or she should live. Each individual should choose what is true/false or right/wrong.
	Authenticity	Individuals should be true to themselves. They should decide in accordance with their personalities.
	Absurdity of Life	Life is meaningless. As such, one is free to do whatever one decides.
	Anxiety or Angst	The sense of complete responsibility which belongs to individuals who must choose for themselves.
	Responsibility	The individual must take responsibility for his life and his situation. To reject responsibility is to act in "bad faith."
Truth	**Subjectivity**	Something is not "true" until you appropriate it for yourself. Truth is dependent upon experience.
Morality	**Subjectivity**	Existentialist ethics are deontological and non-consequentialist. The rule of existentialist ethics is "be true to yourself." In other words, do not let others constrain your actions.
Types of existentialism	**Christian**	Existentialism began with Søren Kierkegaard. He attempted to move the church towards an experiential faith. He was followed by neo-orthodox theologians like Karl Barth, Rudolf Bultmann, and Emil Brunner.
	Atheistic	German existentialists include Friedrich Nietzsche, who began this approach to existentialism. He was followed by Martin Heidegger, who combined existentialism with phenomenology.
		French existentialists followed Martin Heidegger. They include Maurice Merleau-Ponty, Jean-Paul Sartre, Albert Camus, and Simone de Beauvoir.

Chart 20

The Continental Philosophers

Romanticism

Developed in Germany in reaction to the failure of the enlightenment. It was a movement started by artists, musicians, and poets who emphasized a more holistic approach to knowledge. The romantics believed that nature reflects the forces used by the God of creation. They also believed that nature reveals the meaning of existence.

Sources of Knowledge	Reason	Not a very significant source of knowledge.
	Intuition	Knowledge results from means that we do not understand.
	Feeling	The passions are a guide to what is true.
Selfhood—Results from a subjective process.	Subject (me)	Represents the inner life of the individual. The subject is involved in the creation of the phenomenal realm which appears to be objective. Because of the **subject's** involvement in the creation of this world it is actually a subjective world. The **subject** is involved with nature and the **objects** in it as a result of his sensory experience.
	Object (everything not me)	Represents the outer world of things.

Romanticists

All Romanticist philosophers subscribed to idealism in one form or another.

Johann Gottlieb Fichte 1762–1814	He combined Kant with Romantic thought. In his *Science of Knowledge* he employed Romanticism to support his German nationalism (metaphysical nationalism). He emphasized the uniqueness of German culture.
Friedrich Wilhelm von Schelling 1775–1854	Developed a philosophy of nature based on creative intuition. He believed that the artist was a truer philosopher than the man of pure reason. He also thought that Romantic philosophy could be used as a basis for religious belief.
Friedrich von Schlegel 1772–1829	Classified "progressive universal poetry" and all forms of post-enlightenment artistic expression as "romantisch."
G. W. F. Hegel 1770–1831	History is moving to a state of freedom for mankind. The organic process by which this happens is the (Hegelian) dialectic. Reason is the way that the Absolute (knowledge) can be comprehended. Mind is the only reality.

Chart 21

The Continental Philosophers (continued)

Edmund Husserl's Phenomenology

An **idealistic** and **romantic** approach to epistemology, developed by Edmund Husserl, that attempts to relate acts of consciousness with their objects. It differs from empirical psychology because it's a philosophy that deals with the essence of consciousness.

Acts of Consciousness	**Objects of Consciousness**
Analyzing, judging, imagining, remembering, and willing.	They need not actually exist in reality, but only in the consciousness.

Phenomenological Reduction

1. Get rid of reality.
2. Isolate the **objects of consciousness** and the **acts of consciousness**. There are different types of each.
3. The **transcendental ego** (a self behind the self, the starting point of all knowledge) is the foundation of the **objects of consciousness** and **acts of consciousness**. Husserl equates the **transcendental ego** with **absolute being**. The **transcendental ego** produces the sense that reality exists

Meaning—Arises from interior consciousness.

Martin Heidegger's Phenomenology

While Heidegger said that Husserl gave him the eyes to see, he takes a whole new approach to phenomenology. Heidegger moves from Husserl to Aristotle to develop his view of phenomenological existentialism. In his *Being and Time*, Heidegger uses phenomenology to understand *Dasein* (human existence). He does not see phenomenology as a science, instead Heidegger rejected all philosophical theories.

Heidegger rejects	**Science**	Phenomenology is not a science because *Dasein* is not best approached in scientific terms.
	Husserl's central concepts	Heidegger rejects the transcendental ego, and phenomenological reduction. Consciousness is not the way to understand the connection between humans and the world.
Phenomenology is	***Dasein*** (Human Existence)	Phenomenology is able to understand *Dasein* from within the concrete particularity of a lived life.
	Intentionality	Heidegger agrees with Husserl that intentionality is the defining characteristic of all lived experiences. He disagrees with Husserl that intentionality is the nature of consciousness.
	Alethia (Truth)	Truth according to Heidegger is disclosure, which means the nature of a thing is revealed in our interaction with it.
	Hermeneutics	Heidegger fused phenomenology with hermeneutics. He tied *Dasein* to interpretation because all of our experience is about interpretation. Hermeneutics are about disclosure. Assertion and questioning are key parts of disclosure. Questions can be problematic.

Chart 21

Structuralism and Poststructuralism

Ferdinand Saussure (1857–1913)

Sign	**Signified**	The **signified** is what the sign represents.
	Signifier	The **signifier** is the word that represents the signified.
Arbitrariness		There is no natural connection between the signified and the signifier. Meaning is assigned by the community.
(La) Langue (Language)		The whole linguistic system.
(La) Parole (Speech)		*Parole* must be evaluated by *langue*. Each speech act can be compared to a move in a game of chess. In other words, the structure of a game determines the significance of a move in the same way as the structure of a language gives meaning to a speech act.
Linguistic Relativism		The rejection of both metaphysical and epistemological realism. These are replaced by the belief that we can know only the system of concepts generated by the arbitrary structures of language.
Community		The individual does not have the power to change a sign once the community has determined it.
Semiology		Saussure's study of signs. It includes the study of linguistics and social institutions.

Other Primary Figures

Claude Lévi-Strauss (1908–)
> Applied Saussure's system to anthropology. He asserted that universal truth is found at the level of structure, so he studied social structure in the same way that Saussure studied language.

Roland Barthes (1915–80)
> A literary critic who further developed Saussure's science of semiology. He combined **structuralism** with **existentialism.** He concluded that "the author is dead."

Jacques Lacan (1901–81)
> Applied structuralism to psychoanalysis as well as to sociology and literary criticism. He is also known as a poststructuralist because he challenged the assumption that language is stable.

Michel Foucault (1926–84)
> A philosopher who combined **structuralism** with **existentialism.** He spent most of his work examining the social relationship between the normal and the abnormal.

Chart 22

Premodernity,
Modernity,
and Postmodernity

Premodernity (Before 1600)

Metaphysics *Metaphysics is the primary philosophy in premodernity.*	**Theology**	God exists and everything else is contingent on him.
		The supernatural exists and does not conflict with science.
	Cosmology	God is the first cause and the creator of everything.
	Ontology	**Community**—The individual exists as part of the community, and therefore the community has precedence over the individual.
		Realism—Things exist independent of the observer.
Epistemology *Both empiricism and rationalism were used in premodernity.*	**Correspondence Theory of Truth**	Truth corresponds to reality.
	Epistemological Realism	There is an objective truth that can be known.
	Community	The church views corporately shared beliefs and practices as important. Creeds and traditions are to be adhered to and protected for the good of the community of believers.
	Hermeneutic of Trust	The content of the Bible is without error, infallible, and sufficient.
	Teleological	Epistemology is dependent on metaphysics.
Axiology	**Realism**	Values are real and objective.
	Teleological	Axiology is dependent on metaphysics.
	Community	The rights of the individual are subordinate to the needs of the community.

Chart 23

Modernity (1): (1600–1950)

Epistemology *Epistemology is the primary philosophy in modernity.*	**Individual**	The reasoning individual comes before the community as a legitimate source of knowledge.
	Correspondence Theory of Truth	Truth corresponds to reality. The **British empiricists** (→ 25) held this position. They allowed the use of both inductive and deductive logic.
	Coherence Theory of Truth	Truth results from a coherent system of beliefs that may or may not correspond to reality. The **continental rationalists** (→ 26) subscribed to this theory. They allowed deductive logic only as a source for knowledge.
	Deontological	Epistemology does not depend on metaphysics.
	Hermeneutic of Doubt	Science and reason are to be trusted over the Bible. The supernatural is rejected.
Axiology	**Deontological**	Values do not depend on metaphysics.
	Irrealism	After David Hume. The **British empiricists** believed that values are man-made and subjective. Values depend on rule or laws. These values are still useful.
	Realism	**Continental rationalists** believed in moral facts.
	Individual	Individual rights take precedence over the community.
Metaphysics	**Theology**	God's existence is in doubt.
	Cosmology	Science explains everything in the world.
	Ontology	The **British empiricists** held to realism.
		After Immanuel Kant the **continental rationalists** became idealists.

Chart 24

Modernity (2): British Empiricists and Analytic Philosophers

British Empiricists

Logic	**Deduction**	The empiricists allowed for the use of deduction. David Hume argued that knowledge derived from deduction is trivial.
	Induction	The empiricists allowed for the use of induction. David Hume explained that induction cannot guarantee knowledge.
Epistemology	**Truth**	Correspondence theory of truth.
	Innate Ideas	The British empiricists rejected the possibility of innate ideas.
Metaphysics	**God**	Some (e.g., Berkeley, Reid) thought that belief in God is essential; many did not.
	Cosmology	Cosmology is an essential part of metaphysics.
	Ontology	Ontology is an essential part of metaphysics.
Axiology	**Value**	Ethics and aesthetics are seen as part of the same thing.
	Reason	Moral/aesthetic knowledge does not depend on reason. It comes from a moral/aesthetic sense or from the emotions.

Analytic Philosophers

- Derived from the British empiricists; began in 1903 with G. E. Moore.
- Emphasized Hume's fork.
- Rejected idealism and subjectivism.
- Believed that philosophical problems are largely linguistic problems.
- Emphasized rigorous use of logic.
- Emphasized precision of language.
- Aimed at breaking down complex concepts into their simpler constituents.
- Philosophy of language is first philosophy.

Chart 25

Modernity (3): Continental Rationalists/Continental Philosophers

Continental Rationalists

Logic	**Deduction**	The continental rationalists allowed for the use of deduction because it can provide certainty.
	Induction	Continental rationalists rejected the use of induction because it cannot provide certainty.
Epistemology	**Cartesian Certainty**	Cartesian certainty is absolute certainty of knowledge. This is achieved via **methodological doubt**, which rejects any knowledge of which one is not certain.
	Innate Ideas	Continental rationalists accepted innate ideas.
	Truth	Continental rationalists held to the coherence theory of truth.
Metaphysics	**Cartesianism**	Metaphysical dualism. Everything is either mind or body.
	Ontology	Existence is the only part of metaphysics of which one can be certain.
Axiology	**Value**	Ethics and aesthetics are two separate disciplines.
	Deontology	Axiology is separated from metaphysics.

Continental Philosophy

- Began at the end of the Enlightenment (the Age of Reason), after Kant.
- Began with Johan Gottlieb Fichte.
- Emphasized Romanticism (the belief that knowledge results from intuition and feelings).
- Emphasized idealism and subjectivism.
- Resulted in existentialism.
- Resulted in phenomenology.
- Phenomenology/existentialism was followed by structuralism.

Chart 26

Postmodernity (1950–Present)

Epistemology *Epistemology is still the primary philosophy, but reason and science cannot deliver knowledge.*	**Irrealism**	There is no objective truth to be known.
	Community	The power of the community determines knowledge.
	Pragmatic Theory of Truth	Truth is what works. Truth is subjective.
	Hermeneutic of Suspicion	The author is "dead" and has no rights over the text. Meaning is determined by the power of the community.
Axiology	**Community**	The power of the community determines beauty and morality.
	Nihilism	There is no objective morality or beauty. There is only what is of use to the community.
Metaphysics	**Ontology**	Idealism: the existence of a thing is dependent on the observer.
	Theology	Accepts the possibility of the supernatural. Also accepts the possibility of a plurality of gods.

Philosophical Postmodernity

Postmodernists reduce epistemology and axiology to hermeneutics. They reduce metaphysics to ontology. Postmodernists believe that there is no objective truth or knowledge but rather that there are only interpretations (hermeneutics). Postmodernists also believe that truth and knowledge are determined by power. Postmodernity results from combining existentialism, phenomenology, pragmatism, and structuralism/poststructuralism.

Cultural Postmodernity

Just as there is a philosophical postmodernity, there is also a cultural postmodernity. Cultural postmodernity arrived at about the same time as philosophical postmodernity, in the 1950s. Cultural postmodernity is a Western phenomenon in which people argue that truth is relative because so many different cultures and religions coexist within the same country. Like philosophical postmodernity, cultural postmodernity emphasizes the importance of one's community to determine truth, morality, and beauty. Another aspect of cultural postmodernity is that culture has changed from orality in the premodern worldview, to literacy in the modern worldview, to visual orientation in the postmodern worldview. This resulted from poor reading skills and short attention spans. Television and other visual media are at least partially to blame for both of these trends.

Chart 27

APPROACHES
TO
ETHICS

Metaethics

Metaethics

The Foundations of Morality

Metaphysics of Morals *What is the nature of morality?*	**The Status of Moral Facts**	Are there objective moral facts that exist independent of the observer? If not, then is there any objective value to morality?
	Free Will vs. Determinism	Concerned with moral culpability. Are humans free to act on their own, or is their action predetermined by God? Is there a mediating position?
	Moral Language	Concerned with whether or not there is an objective moral reality and the nature of moral language.
	Moral Properties	Explores the existence of moral properties. It is also concerned with the nature of moral properties.
Moral Epistemology *How is morality known?*	**Cognitivism**	Moral knowledge is gained via a cognitive process.
	Noncognitivism	Moral knowledge is gained via emotions. It assumes that there are no objective moral facts. Nonetheless, this position asserts that morality is still useful.
	Intuition	Moral knowledge is gained via some unknown or undefined means.
Moral Psychology *What is the nature of the moral self?*	**Moral Motivation**	Explores the relationship between moral facts and moral motivation.
	Moral Development	Investigates how people develop morally.
	Mental Health	Explores the relationship between morality and mental health.

Chart 28

The Fact/Value Dichotomy

- Idea started with David Hume and was employed by analytic philosophers like G. E. Moore (1873–1958).
- This dichotomy has its roots in Hume's fork. Truth is either analytic (necessary and deducible values) or synthetic (empirically verifiable facts).
- Values are evaluated by the passions and facts are evaluated by reason.
- It asserts that "one cannot derive ought from is." In other words, values (ethics and aesthetics) have nothing to do with metaphysics.
- All supposed connections between ethics and metaphysics are based only on induction.
- Both ethics and aesthetics are based solely on emotions.
- This dichotomy rejects teleology, natural law, and any idea of moral properties.
- This implies that values have no significance for science, economics, law, political theory, or psychology.

W. V. O. Quine (1908–2000) argued that the analytic/synthetic distinction is faulty. Consequently, the fact/value dichotomy collapsed with the analytic/synthetic distinction.

Chart 29

Metaphysics of Morals

The Nature of Morality

Moral Facts	**Realism**	Moral facts are found and not made by humans. They exist independent of the observer.
	Irrealism	Moral facts are created and not found by humans, but morality is useful for a successful society.
	Nihilism	Moral facts do not exist, and morality is not even useful.
Moral Properties	Naturalism	Moral properties are identical to natural properties.
	Eliminativism	This reductionistic approach asserts that there are no moral properties.
	Supervenience	Moral properties are relationally dependent on other properties.
	Essentialism	This view of moral properties is similar to naturalism but allows for the possibility of the supernatural. Moral properties depend on the essence of a thing. Essentialism assumes that the essence of a thing carries an intrinsic and objective value. It examines morality in all possible worlds.
Moral Language	**Emotivism**	A view of morality developed by the analytic philosopher A. J. Ayer (1910–89). He asserted that moral statements are nothing more than primitive, emotional noise. Moral statements are meaningless because there is no such thing as morality; there are only emotions.
	Prescriptivism	A view developed by the analytic philosopher Richard Hare (1919–2002). Moral language has a logic of its own. Moral language is more than just primitive emotions. It is instead more of a command. For example, to say that stealing is immoral means "Don't steal." Morality is thus about rules. These moral commands are universal, but they are not specific.
Moral Responsibility	**Freedom**	Individual moral agents are morally culpable for their actions because they are free to do as they wish.
	Compatibilism	Individual moral agents have limited moral culpability for their actions because their wills are only partially free.
	Determinism	Individual moral agents do not have free will because of God, biology, or other external forces. Some hold that in this case moral agents are still morally culpable, others that the moral agents are not morally culpable.

Chart 30

Moral Epistemology

How Morality Is Known

Cognitivism *Assumes that moral facts are found and not made. Morality is objective.*	**Internalism** *Moral knowledge is like other kinds of knowledge. Knowledge is justified true belief.*	**Foundationalism**—Moral knowledge is dependent on a foundation of knowledge that is properly basic.
		Coherentism—Moral knowledge relies on a system of coherent beliefs.
	Externalism *Moral knowledge is like other kinds of knowledge. Knowledge results from a reliable belief-forming process or mechanism.*	**Naturalized Epistemology**—Moral knowledge results from natural processes, perhaps a moral sense.
		Virtue Epistemology—Moral knowledge results from the use of virtues such as prudence.
		Proper Functionalism—Moral knowledge results when a normal healthy person functions as he or she should. This may involve the use of naturalized epistemology or virtue epistemology.
Noncognitivism *Assumes that moral facts are made and not found Morality is subjective.*	**Intuitionism**	Moral knowledge results from an undefined means.
	Emotivism	There is no such thing as objective morality. Instead, morality is mere public opinion. To say that something is good is merely to mean that one likes that thing. To say that something is bad means that one dislikes that thing. Hence, morality is nothing more than emotional preference.

Chart 31

Moral Psychology (1)

The Nature of the Moral Self

Moral Motivation (also → 33)	**Internalism** *Recognition of moral facts provides motivation for moral action.*	**Weak Internalism**—Moral facts provide some motivation for moral action.
		Strong Internalism—Moral facts provide sufficient motivation for moral action.
	Externalism	The rejection of **internalism.**
	Altruism	**Genuine Altruism**—Acts are done for the benefit of others.
		Pseudo-Altruism—Acts that benefit others are performed to satisfy one's own desires.
	Egoism	**Rational Egoism**—Amoral agents have reason to act in a way that is consistent with their own self-interest.
		Psychological Egoism—A statement of the way that human nature is. An agent acts only to promote his own self-interest.
		Ethical Egoism—States what people ought to do. Agents should act to promote their own self-interest.
	Welfarism	**Objectivism**—Asserts that the well-being of an agent is not a matter of the agent's attitudes or preferences. Instead, well-being depends on some external standard.
		Subjectivism—Asserts that the well-being of an agent is a matter of the agent's attitudes or preferences.
		Hybrid—Asserts that some aspects of an agent's well-being depend on the agent's attitudes or preferences and some do not.
Moral Development	**Cognitivism**	An approach to moral development endorsed by **internalists** in which moral agents regulate themselves.
	Noncognitivism	A view of moral development held by **externalists** in which the moral agent is regulated by others.
Moral Health	**Welfarism**	Asserts that if one is healthy, he or she will recognize and be motivated by moral facts. It assumes that the moral person is a happy person.
	Positivism	Asserts that there is no connection between recognition of moral facts and mental health.

Chart 32

Moral Psychology (2): Moral Motivation

Emotion is a factor

Some philosophers/ethicists believe that emotions are judgments of value and motivate us to take action.

Emotion is not a factor

Some philosophers/ethicists believe that emotions are irrational.

Internalism

Asserts that the recognition of moral facts provides motivation for moral action.

Externalism

A rejection of internalism. The recognition of moral facts provides no motivation for moral action.

These perspectives can be combined in four ways:

	Emotion *is* a factor	Emotion is *not* a factor
Internalism	**Welfarism** *The claim that the primary reasons for action are aspects of well-being, which result in eudaimonia (the happiness resulting from self-effort).* **Promotionism** *The claim that the only reasons for action are aspects of well-being to be promoted.*	**Duty** *The only reasons for action are obligations.*
Externalism	**Hedonistic Instrumentalism** *Morality is useful only as it relates to pleasure and pain.*	**Amoralism** *The belief that morality is a sham and is not even useful.* *or* **Instrumentalism** *Moral facts may or may not exist, but morality is useful.*

The Major Problem in Moral Psychology

- Most moral philosophers are moral realists.
- Most moral philosophers subscribe to motivational internalism.
- Most psychologists are moral irrealists.
- Most psychologists subscribe to motivational externalism.
- Only motivational internalists believe in a conscience and believe that mental health is affected by moral development.
- There is also confusion regarding the function of emotions: some believe that emotions are judgments of value, others, that emotions are simply irrational bodily feelings.

Chart 33

Internalist Moral Development (Cognitivism)

Jean Piaget (1896–1980)

One of a few significant psychologists who agreed with moral philosophers. Piaget believed that recognition of moral facts does provide motivation for moral action. He also believed that there are two stages of moral development.

Stage 1	The Heteronomous Stage	Moral agents learn moral values from others.
Stage 2	The Autonomous Stage	Moral agents adopt the moral standards that they were brought up with.

Lawrence Kohlberg (1927–87)

The other significant psychologist who agreed with moral philosophers. He took Piaget's ideas and developed them into a more sophisticated system. He believed that a deontological ethical theory was most consistent with his theory of moral development.

Preconventional Level	Stage 1	Punishment and obedience. A person does right because it affects his or her well-being.
	Stage 2	A person learns to balance self-interest with the interests of others.
Conventional Level	Stage 3	Conformity—expectations of others become important. Doing right requires adhering to expectations of those one loves and respects.
	Stage 4	Social system and conscience maintenance. One does right because it fulfills his or her institutional duties and obligations. Some people may not progress beyond this stage.
Postconventional and Principled Level	Stage 5	Social contract ethical principles are adhered to because everyone accepts them.
	Stage 6	Universal ethical principles are adhered to because they are right.

Chart 34

Externalist Moral Development (Noncognitivism)

According to Thomas Wren (*Caring about Morality*), externalist approaches to moral development emphasize socialization theories. These approaches all emphasize heteronomy (the idea that people regulate their behavior because they fear external sources).

Noncognitive Moral Psychologies	**Radical Behaviorism**	An approach developed by B. F. Skinner (1904–90). It assumes that the good is whatever society determines it to be.
	Chaining and External Markers	An approach to moral development based on behaviorism.
	Psychological Contagion	Imitative behavior (intentionally or unintentionally) because of some affect-arousing feature in a person or in his or her behavior.
Semicognitive Moral Psychologies *These theories assume some kind of "war of the passions" that can be resolved in a number of ways.*	**Approach Avoidance Theory**	An approach developed by Kurt Lewin (1890–1947) and Neal Miller (1909–). Conflict is envisioned as a competition of desires (or moral motives). The strongest of these desires is what ultimately causes a person to act in one way or another. These desires are tempered by fear of punishment.
	Cathexis Theory of Conflict Resolution	An approach based on Freud's theory of repression. Cathexis is the idea of psychic energy channeled into an object. Improper desires should be channeled into another object to repress them.
	Modeling and Vicarious Reinforcement	An approach developed by Alfred Bandura (1925–). It assumes that correct moral behavior can be acquired through modeling. Such modeling involves vicarious experience through observation. The moral agent must also consider the consequence of the model's actions to reinforce what he or she has learned.

Chart 35

Normative Ethics

Normative Ethics

Key Terms

Teleology	1. Ethics depends on metaphysics. 2. Goodness depends on being. 3. Pursuit of the good. 4. The good depends on the nature of a thing. 5. The good determines what is right.
Deontology	1. Ethics has no relation to metaphysics. 2. Rules determine what is right. 3. Right determines what is good. 4. Ethics are only obligations to rules or laws. 5. Rightness has priority over the good.
Consequentialism	1. To maximize the good. 2. The good depends on the consequences of an action instead of metaphysics. 3. The outcome is primary. 4. The end justifies the means. 5. Rightness has priority over the good.
Nonconsequentialism	A rejection of consequentialism.
Act	Rightness is determined by the action that one should take.
Rule	Rightness is determined only by rules or laws.

Major Ethical Theories

Teleology	Deontology	
	Act Consequentialism Contractarianism Act Utilitarianism Virtue Consequentialism	**Rule Consequentialism** Contractualism Rule Utilitarianism
Naturalism		
Virtue Ethics	**Act Non-Consequentialism** Existentialism Situational Ethics Moral Particularism Linguistic Virtue Ethics	**Rule Non-Consequentialism** Kantianism Rossian Intuitionism Divine Command Theory

Teleological virtue ethics requires naturalism, but naturalism does not require virtue ethics.

Both moral particularism and situational ethics suggest that moral principles and practical reasoning are insufficient to make good moral judgments. Each case is unique and should be judged on its own merits.

Chart 36

Virtue Ethics

Essential Components	**Natural Law**	A kind of naturalism that suggests that ethical properties are identical to natural properties. Right and wrong are based on the nature of a thing. Virtues are what make a thing good. Virtue ethics are based on human nature. Aristotle argued that the natural law is universal, rational, and objective. Natural law points to the existence of God, who establishes the created order. God also determines what is good and right.
	Doctrine of the Mean	The idea that there is a continuum of behavior. Virtue is in the middle of this continuum. A deficiency of a virtue is a vice, an excess of a virtue is also a vice.
	Perfectionism	Virtues emphasize human excellence.
	Welfarism	To act in accordance with virtue is in a moral agent's best interest. The virtuous person is a happier person.
Types of Virtue Ethics	**Aristotelian Virtue Ethics (Classical)**	A premodern system of ethics focused on character and natural law. The person of character acts in accordance with the natural law. The virtues of humans are determined by this natural law (or the nature of a thing). The virtuous person gains happiness (*eudaimonia*—happiness gained by self effort). One gains character by watching someone who already has character. One may also gain character by listening to or reading narratives.
	Augustinian Virtue Ethics	A premodern system of Christian ethics. The natural (cardinal) virtues are insufficient to provide true happiness, in contrast to beatitude, happiness from God. Only the Christian can have hope of beatitude. The Holy Spirit infuses the theological virtues into the believer. The believer gains the cardinal virtues *after* the theological virtues.
	Agent-Based	A modern system of virtue ethics developed by analytic philosophers. It is a system that has no place for natural law.
	Linguistic Virtue Ethics	A postmodern approach to virtue ethics developed by Alasdair MacIntyre (1929–) and based on the ideas of Ludwig Wittgenstein (1889–1951). It emphasizes the importance of narrative and community. It rejects moral, epistemological, and metaphysical realism.

Chart 37

Aristotelian (Classical) Virtue Ethics

Aristotle's ethical theory is found in his *Nichomachean Ethics, Eudomean Ethics, Magna Moralia,* and *The Politics.* He assumes metaphysical and epistemological realism. Civil law should be based on natural law.

Metaethical Presuppositions	**Metaphysics of Morals**	**Moral Realism**—Moral facts exist independent of the observer. Moral facts are found and not made.
		Free Will—Humans are free to act as they choose.
	Moral Epistemology	**Cognitivism**—Moral knowledge results from the use of the virtue of prudence (Gk. *phronesis*).
	Moral Psychology	**Motivational Internalism**—Recognition of moral facts does provide motivation for moral action.
		Cognitive Moral Development—A person begins life as an egoist, but as that person matures he or she becomes more altruistic.
		Mental Health—One cannot be happy without being virtuous.
Cardinal Virtues[1]	**Justice**	Because humans are social creatures, this is the most important virtue.
	Prudence	= Practical wisdom. This is a special virtue because it is both an intellectual virtue and a moral virtue.
	Courage	This is an ability to overcome fear. It allows one to do what must be done even in difficult circumstances.
	Temperance	= Self-control. This is an ability to delay gratification, because to succumb to one's desire may be detrimental to one's well-being.
Types of Character[2]	**Superhuman Virtue**	A person does the right thing because he desires to do what is right.
	Continent Man	A person does the right thing even when he does not desire to do so.
	Virtuous Man	Is governed by prudence and temperance.
	Vicious Man	Lacks prudence and temperance.
	Incontinent Man	Does wrong because he is ruled by his passions.
	Brutish Man	Does wrong and is unrepentant over his actions.

1. These virtues are based on natural law (human nature) and are required for everyone. One's employment and position will require some of these more than others.
2. Aristotle believed that people act viciously only when they lack knowledge (training) or power.

Chart 38

Augustinian Virtue Ethics

Augustine assumed metaphysical but not epistemological realism. Thomas Aquinas and Bonaventure assume both metaphysical and epistemological realism.

Metaethical Presuppositions	**Metaphysics of Morals**	**Moral Realism**—Moral facts exist independent of the observer. Moral facts are found and not made.
		The Good—God is the greatest and highest good.
		Predestination—After Pelagius, Augustine held to a strong view of election and moral culpability.
	Moral Epistemology	Augustine is not clear on how one knows morality, but Scripture reading is essential. Aquinas explains that the conscience is composed of a moral faculty (*synderesis*) plus reasoning (the virtue of prudence).
	Moral Psychology *The believer can do acts of supererogation. The believer can have the character of the person of superhuman virtue.*	**Motivational Internalism**—Recognition of moral facts does provide motivation for moral action.
		Moral Development—Before salvation this is irrelevant. After salvation one goes through the process of sanctification.
		Mental Health—Before salvation one does not function properly. Sin causes a kind of insanity. Happiness (*eudaimonia*, the happiness that comes from self-effort) is fleeting. After salvation one can achieve true happiness (*makarios*, the happiness that comes from God).
Theological Virtues *Created in the believer by the Holy Spirit giving him the power and knowledge to live righteously.*	**Love** Gk. *agape* Lat. *caritas*	The love of God and the love of others for God's sake. This is the primary virtue that unifies all of the other virtues, whether theological, moral, or intellectual. Its opposite is *cupiditas* (Lat., "self-love").
	Faith	Grows out of love and gives one spiritual knowledge.
	Hope	Grows out of love and causes one to look at eternity.
Cardinal Virtues	The cardinal virtues are added to the person with the theological virtues. If one does not have the theological virtues, then one's virtues are only excellent vices.	
Eternal Law	All of God's laws by which he governs the universe. It existed before time began. Some argue that it is God himself.	
	Divine Law	The Old and the New Testament.
	Natural Law	General revelation makes known to all the morality of the Ten Commandments.
Temporal Law	**Civil Law**	Natural law should serve as the foundation for civil law. This law is man-made and should encourage virtue.

Chart 39

Linguistic Virtue Ethics

This postmodern approach to ethics was developed by Alasdair MacIntyre (1929–). His most significant works are *After Virtue, Whose Justice, Which Morality*, and *Three Rival Versions of Moral Inquiry*. MacIntyre subscribes to Thomas Aquinas's list of virtues because he combines the virtues of Augustine with the virtues of Aristotle. He was influenced by the thought of Ludwig Wittgenstein (1889–1951), who rejected metaphysics and replaced it with linguistic analysis. Consequently, MacIntyre leaves no place for natural law or what he calls "metaphysical biology." Stanley Hauerwas (1940–) has followed after MacIntyre's ethical theory. They are also metaphysical nominalists, rejecting the existence of universals.

Metaethical Presuppositions	**Metaphysics of Morals**	**Moral Irrealism**—Morality is important because of the community.
		Free Will—Humans are morally culpable because they are free.
	Moral Epistemology	**Cognitivism**—Moral knowledge is gained through the virtue prudence.
	Moral Psychology	**Motivational Internalism**
		Cognitive Moral Development
		Welfarism
Theological Virtues *(Augustine)*	**Love**	The love of God and the love of others for God's sake.
	Faith	Grows out of love and gives one spiritual knowledge.
	Hope	Grows out of love and causes a person to look at eternity.
Cardinal Virtues *(Aristotle)*	**Justice**	The most important social virtue.
	Prudence	Practical wisdom, a key to moral judgment.
	Courage	The ability to overcome fear.
	Temperance	Self-control.
Community	The community is important because it determines meaning, truth, and morality. The individual must operate by the preestablished rules of the community.	
Narrative	Narrative is the key to learning of any type—especially for learning moral character.	
Language	We are surrounded by language and cannot understand without it.	

Chart 40

Deontology

Divine Command Theory	A metaethical theory that argues that moral facts are based on God's will. It is also a normative theory that argues the will of God is authoritative. God's commands are to be obeyed.
Kantianism	A modern ethical theory that emphasizes universalizability and equitability.
Intuitionism	An approach to ethics developed by the analytic philosopher W. D. Ross (1877–1940). It posits a hierarchy of laws that must be obeyed.
Graded Absolutism	An approach developed by Norman Geisler (1932) that posits a hierarchy of laws that must be obeyed.

Deontology arose in the modern period, following the ideas of William of Ockham (1287–1347/49). Ockham was a proponent of divine command theory who separated God's will from God's nature. Thus Ockham separated ethics from metaphysics.

The continental rationalist (→ 26) approach to ethics was exemplified by Immanuel Kant. The continental philosophers (→ 26) were deontological as well.

The ethics of the British empiricists (→ 25) was exemplified by David Hume, who argued that "one cannot derive ought from is" (the fact/value dichotomy [→ 29]). The ethics of the British empiricists was consequentialist. As such, they were deontological. The analytic philosophers (→ 25) were deontological until G. E. M. Anscombe (1919–2001) urged a return to premodern ethics.

Chart 41

Divine Command Theory (Theological Voluntarism)

John Duns Scotus (1266–1308)	Argued that goodness is based on God's will and God's nature. Suggested that God's will is consistent with his nature. Both natural law and virtue ethics are compatible with this version of divine command theory.
William Ockham (1285–1347/49)	Wanted to emphasize the freedom of God. He asserted that goodness is based only on God's will. This version of divine command theory is compatible only with deontological ethical theories. As such, it is vulnerable to Plato's **Euthyphro Dilemma** (see below).
The Euthyphro Dilemma	The Euthyphro Dilemma has two parts: 1. If something is good because God declares it so, then goodness is arbitrary. 2. If, on the other hand, God approves of something because it is good, then goodness is something apart from God.

Divine Command Metaethics

Metaphysics of Morals	**The Good**	Moral facts are based upon God's will. To be or do good is to act in accordance with the will of God. Natural law is in accordance with God's will. Virtue ethics can be consistent with divine command theory.
Moral Epistemology	**The Noetic Effects of Sin**	Man is so constructed by God that moral knowledge is inherent. Because of sin moral knowledge is confused. Consequently, moral knowledge results from hearing the Word of God.
Moral Psychology	**Internalism**	Moral knowledge provides motivation for moral action.
	Mental Health	Moral action results in *eudaimonia*.

Chart 42

Kantian Deontology

This approach was developed by Immanuel Kant in his *Groundwork for a Metaphysics of Morals, Critique of Practical Reason,* and *Metaphysics of Morals.*

Metaethical Presuppositions	Metaphysics of Morals	**Moral Realism**—Moral facts exist independent of the observer. Moral facts are found and not made.
		The Good—An action done from a good will.
		Free Will—Humans are morally culpable for their actions.
	Moral Epistemology	**Cognitivism**—Morality is known through the use of practical reason alone. The Bible is not needed.
	Moral Psychology	**Motivational Internalism**
		Cognitive Moral Development
		Positivism—Virtue and happiness are not united in this life.
Respect for Persons	Because every person is endowed with the ability to think and choose, all people should be treated with respect.	
Equality	All people should have an equal opportunity to attain whatever status they desire in a free society.	
Universality	The laws of society should apply to everyone.	
Hypothetical Imperative	Concerns all of the possible situations one might find oneself in. They are infinite in number, so there is an infinite number of possible commands.	
Categorical Imperative These are concerned with intrinsic goods. It has two functions: **Function 1:** to obligate the moral agent to obey. **Function 2:** to act as a test of moral maxims.	**1. Autonomy**	One should never act in such a way that one could not also will that one's maxim should be a universal law.
	2. Respect for Persons	Always treat humanity as an end and never as a means.
	3. Legislation for a Moral Community	All maxims that proceed from one's own making of law ought to harmonize with a possible moral community.
Conclusion Kant believed that virtue and happiness cannot be united in this life.	1. God exists, and we should worship him. 2. There is objective right and wrong. 3. There is an afterlife. 4. There is a postmortem judgment. 5. God will reward the good and punish the evil in the next life.	

Chart 43

Deontological Intuitionism

W. D. Ross (1877–1940) was primarily concerned with metaethics. He explained what he thought was the dominant ethical theory of the nineteenth century in *The Right and the Good*. This view is also known as Rossian Intuitionism.

Metaethical Presuppositions	**Metaphysics of Morals**	**Moral Realism**
		The Good—unexplained.
		Free Will
	Moral Epistemology	**Noncognitivism**—Moral knowledge is intuited. Moral principles are self-evident.
	Moral Psychology	**Motivational Internalism**
		Cognitivism
Other Presuppositions	Moral principles cannot be reduced to, or unified into, general principles.	
	Moral principles are absolute.	
	Ethics are deontological.	
	Ethical conflicts are resolved through a hierarchy of laws.	
7 Prima Facie Duties	**Promise Keeping**—One must always keep one's promises under any condition.	
	Fidelity—One should always be loyal and true to one's family and friends.	
	Gratitude—One should always be thankful for what others have done for him or her.	
	Goodwill—One's actions should always be motivated by goodwill.	
	Justice—One should always strive to act justly and see that justice is carried out.	
	Self-Improvement—One should never be content with one's character and should always strive to improve.	
	Nonmalificence—One should always strive to control one's actions so that one does not act out of evil intent.	

Chart 44

Graded Absolutism (Hierarchicalism)

Norman Geisler presents this moral theory in *Ethics: Alternatives and Issues*. Geisler asserts that Augustine and Charles Hodge held to this moral theory.

Metaethical Presuppositions	Metaphysics of Morals	Moral Realism
		The Good—Depends on God's will.
		Free Will
	Moral Epistemology	Cognitivism
	Moral Psychology	Motivational Internalism
		Cognitivism
Other Presuppositions	According to Geisler, "God is one in nature, but he has many moral attributes. Each absolute moral law is traceable to one of God's unchangeable moral attributes."	
	Christian ethics are deontological.	
	Ethical conflicts are resolved by use of a hierarchy of laws. Avoid the greater evil by doing the lesser.	
	Graded absolutism recognizes moral absolutes.	
	Graded absolutism should not be confused with utilitarianism.	
	Graded absolutism should not be confused with situational ethics.	
	Graded absolutism recognizes **exemptions** from but not **exceptions** to absolute moral laws. • Geisler argues that "**exceptions** violate the universality and absoluteness of a moral law." • An **exemption** only eliminates the individual's culpability of breaking a lower law while still recognizing absolute moral laws.	
Geisler's Hierarchy	1. Love for God over love for man. 2. Obey God over government. 3. Mercy over veracity.	

Chart 45

Act Utilitarianism

eremy Bentham (1748–1832) modified the utilitarianism of Francis Hutcheson (1694–1746) and David Hume 1711–76). It is a system that is teleological and consequentialist. It is a hedonistic (focused on pleasure) pproach to ethics. Bentham believed that it is better to be "a satisfied pig than a dissatisfied Socrates."

Metaethical Presuppositions	**Metaphysics of Morals**	**Moral Realism**
		The Good—Pleasure or happiness.
		Free Will
	Moral Epistemology	**Noncognitivism**—The passions (emotions) act as a moral sense.
	Moral Psychology	**Motivational Externalism**
		Noncognitivism
		Positivism—Happiness is equated with pleasure. There is no objective good to be united with virtue.
Greatest Happiness Principle	Act utilitarianism provides the greatest amount of happiness for the greatest number of people.	
Explanation	An act is right if it results in as much good as any other alternative.	
Calculus of Happiness	Decisions are based on the total amount of pleasure to be gained minus the total amount of pain to be experienced. The calculus of happiness (or hedonic calculus) takes into consideration: • the number of people to experience the pleasure or pain • the certainty of the pleasure or pain • the intensity of the pleasure or pain • the duration of the pleasure or pain • the frequency of the pleasure or pain	
Political Theory	A democracy is the best form of government because it is the most compatible with utilitarianism.	

Chart 46

Rule Utilitarianism

John Stuart Mill developed this ethical system in response to the weaknesses of act utilitarianism. Mill believed that it is better to be Socrates dissatisfied than a pig satisfied. This system is deontological and consequentialist.

Metaethical Presuppositions	**Metaphysics of Morals**	Moral Irrealism
		The Good—Happiness (*eudaimonia*).
		Free Will
	Moral Epistemology	Noncognitivism
	Moral Psychology	Motivational Externalism
		Noncognitivism
		Welfarism
Happiness	Happiness (*eudaimonia*) is more than pleasure. It involves higher-order pleasures such as intellectual and aesthetic enjoyment.	
Definition of Rule Utilitarianism	The rightness of an act does not depend on its consequences. An act is right if and only if it is required by a code of rules whose acceptance would lead to the greater utility for society than any available alternative.	
Code of Rules	These rules ensure that a minimally correct standard of behavior is enforced and encouraged.	
Universality	The set of rules must apply to everyone.	

Chart 47

Contractarianism

This approach was developed by Thomas Hobbes (1588–1670) and Jean-Jacques Rousseau (1712–78). Contractarianism is an ethical system that is deontological and consequentialist. It is both an ethical and a political theory.

Metaethical Presuppositions	**Metaphysics of Morals**	Irrealism
		The Good—Whatever brings peace and order. What is right to do depends on what rules it would be in everyone's interest for all to accept.
		Free Will
	Moral Epistemology	Motivational Externalism
	Moral Psychology	Motivational Externalism
		Noncognitivism
		Welfarism
Man's State of Nature	According to Thomas Hobbes, "Man's natural state is a state of war of all against all." If left to himself, man's life is "solitary, poor, nasty, brutish and short." Man is free, equal, and rational, but he is also egoistic and antisocial.	
Solution	**The State**	A strong state is the only way to protect humans from each other. Every citizen owes total allegiance to the state, because the state offers humans protection from each other. The state is legitimate as long as it can demonstrate itself capable of exercising power.
	Social Contract	People are born into society and are automatically enrolled in the social contract. This contract is something that all rational and competent agents would agree to. People have no way to get out of this contract. Thus they must obey the state.
	Rights	Humans have few rights, and even these are subject to the needs of the state.
	Rules/Laws	People must forgo the pursuit of their own interests to obey the rules that promote the interests of society as a whole.

Chart 48

Contractualism

This position was developed by Immanuel Kant and, most recently, by John Rawls (1921–2002). Like contractarianism, it is a deontological and consequentialist ethical and political theory.

Metaethical Presuppositions	**Metaphysics of Morals**	**Realist**—Moral facts are found and not made.
		The Good—Determined by what is right. All rational people can conclude what is right and will agree to it.
		Free Will
	Moral Epistemology	Cognitivist
	Moral Psychology	**Motivational Internalism**
		Cognitivism
		Welfarism
Man's State of Nature	People are rational and equal. At the same time, they are also antisocial and egoistic.	
	The State	The state is agreed to by all competent rational individuals for the good of all.
	The Social Contract	The social contract is a device used to reveal what is moral.
	Rights	All people have equal rights.
	Rules/Laws	Rules and laws are understood as something that rational individuals would agree to from a common perspective as one free and equal person among others.
	Virtue	According to John Rawls, **justice** is the primary virtue. He asserts that justice is fairness.

Chart 49

Applied Ethics

Political Philosophy

Morality and the State	**Welfarism**	The state has the function of looking after the welfare of its people.
	Perfectionism	The promotion of human excellence is a primary factor in the evaluation of the political and social worth of a society. This assumes that there is a distinctive human nature.
	Positivism	Political philosophy has nothing to do with morality.
Types of Government *(According to Aristotle)*	**Benevolent Monarchy**	According to Aristotle, this is the best kind of government.
	Aristocracy	The rule of the best.
	Polity	The rule of citizens.
	Democracy	The rule of the many.
	Oligarchy	The rule of the few.
	Tyranny	The worst kind of government.
Political Positions	**Liberal**	**Classical liberals** emphasize personal freedom and individual rights. These rights include the right to life, liberty, and property. They desire to limit the power of the state.
		Modern liberals emphasize the freedoms of the French Revolution: liberty, equality, and fraternity. This position rejects social morality.
		Radicals desire dramatic and immediate change.
	Moderate	**Moderates** believe that the best position is one that avoids extremes.
	Conservative	**Libertarians** are fiscally conservative but desire no interference from the government.
		Communitarians emphasize the individual's duties to society.
		Reactionaries believe that things have changed too much and desire to change things back.
Philosophy of Law	Concerned with the nature and purpose of law. Every society has some kind of legal system to resolve conflict and to make sure that justice is carried out.	
Economics	The study of wealth and poverty of societies and of individuals. Aristotle believed that economics is prior to politics.	

Chart 50

Philosophy of Law

Theories of Justice	**Retributive**	Ensures that those who violate the laws of society receive the punishment that is their due.
	Distributive	The fair arrangement of goods, benefits, and responsibilities in society.
Legal Theory	**Natural Law**	Classical view of natural law based on metaphysical presuppositions that asserts that there is a higher law that serves as a basis for civil law. The contemporary views of natural law are contrasted with legal positivism. Contemporary natural law theory asserts that there is a moral aspect to every law that should show the validity of that law. Natural rights are based on the idea of natural law.
	Legal Positivism	Nineteenth-century idea that asserts that laws are only social constructs of a given society. Also asserts that there is no connection between law and morality.
	Law and Economics	Asserts that economic principles apply to every legal problem. This includes such things as family law, criminal law, and tort law.
	Postmodernism	Concerned with how lawyers use language and how language relates to truth. This includes the study of feminism and the law, deconstruction, and pragmatism.
Areas of Law	**Business Law**	Includes such things as property law, contract law, and tort law.
	Criminal Law	Is concerned with crime and punishment.
	Constitutional Law	Is concerned with whether a given law is consistent with the constitution of a country.
	International Law	Also called **law of nations**. A set of rules generally regarded and accepted as binding in relations between states and nations.

Chart 51

Economics

Presuppositions	*Homo economicus*	A model of a rational economic human being. This model is egoistic and acts for its own self-interest. This self-interest causes *Homo economicus* to be motivated by incentives.
	Allocation of Scarce Resources	Awareness of this scarcity combined with human self-interest causes changes in prices and behaviors.
	Fair Exchange	Results from people attempting to meet their own desires for scarce resources. Money is used to facilitate this fair exchange for goods and services.
Requirements for Markets	**Property Rights**	Based on natural law. According to Aristotle, property rights are needed for virtue, e.g., liberality and magnanimity.
	Law	Protects property rights and enforces voluntary agreements in contracts.
	The State	The enforcer of the rule of law.
Ethics and Economics	**Positive Economics**	Positive economics is the science that studies human behavior as it attempts to solve the problem of the allocation of scarce resources. It tries to understand how economic activity is affected by changes in economic policy. It is not concerned with ethical judgments concerning the policy or the activity.
	Normative Economics	Normative economics (or political economy) deals with the basic principles for the ethical advancement of the national economy by public officials. Thus the formulation of economic policy is a normative activity.
Types of Economics	**Macroeconomics**	Concerned with national economies.
	Microeconomics	Concerned with economics at the local level.
Economic Theories	**Capitalism**	An economic system in which all or most of the means of production are privately owned and operated for profit. This system assumes that a free market is essential.
	Monetarism	A return to the principles set forth in *The Wealth of Nations* by Adam Smith (1723–90). It is a rejection of the Keynesian approach to economics. This approach was proposed by the Austrian Friedrich A. von Hayek (1899–1992) and adopted in America by Milton Friedman (1912–). It is often referred to as the **Chicago school of economics.**
	Keynesianism	The economic system developed by John Maynard Keynes (1883–1946) in his book *The General Theory of Employment, Interest and Money*. It rejects the laissez-faire free market system that minimizes state intervention. It advocates government intervention to stimulate the level of demand. It also asserts that a small amount of inflation is acceptable to maintain full employment.
	Socialism	A system that developed in opposition to capitalism. It is a form of utopian liberalism that combines interest in social justice with economic reform. As such, it emphasizes the importance of the worker. In many cases, socialism has been combined with **Marxism**, but it is not limited to any one political system.

Chart 52

Adam Smith

In 1776 Adam Smith (1723–90) published *An Inquiry into the Nature and Causes of the Wealth of Nations.* Many consider him to be the father of modern economic theory. Adam Smith was primarily concerned with economic growth and assumed that "men are not angels," that is, we act in our own self-interest, not for the common good. He was concerned with creating an economic system with incentives to act for the common good, because these incentives benefited oneself.

Property Rights	Smith emphasized the efficiency of privately owned property. Private ownership is thus beneficial to society as a whole. He also made clear the inefficiency of state-owned property.
Division of Labor	Smith provided a systematic explanation of the division of labor and its consequences for an economy.
Taxation	Smith asserted that taxation has a negative effect on the economy.

Chart 53

Marxism

Karl Marx (1818–83) and Frederich Engels (1820–95) wrote the *Communist Manifesto* and *Das Kapital*. These works explain a political-economic philosophy that has held much of the world in slavery for the better part of the last century. There is no one agreed-upon system, but rather a family of theories associated with Marxism. Today these theories are viewed as a failure. There are a number of significant components to this family of theories.

Atheism	Marxism subscribes to a metaphysical materialist viewpoint. In this position there is no God, and religion is only an opiate of the masses.
Class Struggle	Marx saw class struggle as an ongoing problem throughout history. Because he was influenced by Hegelian thought, he held a teleological view of history. He believed that history would culminate with the working class overthrowing the ruling class. This socialist revolution would result in the complete liberation of man.
Theory of Society	Marx provided a critical analysis of society. He concluded that economics is the foundation of society and all else is superstructure. He believed that society would evolve from the primitive commune to the social class with a capitalist economy. The last stage of this evolution is a socialist revolution resulting in the elimination of private property and the division of labor.
Science	Marx claimed that this theory was scientific. That is, he believed that history progresses based on an inexorable law. The end of history, the socialist utopia, was inevitable, as certain as the law of gravity or the laws of motion.

Chart 54

Business Ethics

Because business depends on property rights, it is concerned with political, legal, and economic theory. Just as the government should ensure virtue in its citizens by means of law, it should ensure virtue in business as well. A business can use any one of the different ethical theories explained in this chapter.

Ethics in Business Disciplines	**Finance Ethics**	**Financial Markets**—Concerned with regulation of fair and orderly markets.
		Financial Services—Concerned with intermediaries who make decisions for others.
		Financial Management—Concerned with the leadership of companies and their responsibilities to stockholders.
	Accounting Ethics	Concerned with the professional conduct of accountants and those over them.
	Marketing Ethics	Concerned with what is permissible to tell potential purchasers about a product. Also concerned with how information about a product should be conveyed.
	Managerial Ethics	Explores the many aspects of management and its responsibility to its employees and clients.
	Business Ethics and the Social Sciences	The social sciences often accept the fact/value dichotomy. Consequently, some social scientists are only concerned with what morality people have instead of the morals they ought to have.
Issues in Business Ethics	**International Business Ethics**	**Cultural Issues**—Culture is a key feature of morality. What is moral in one country may be seen as immoral in another.
		National Economics—Different nations have different economic systems and standards.
		Globalism—Concerned with what moral standards ought to be used with increasing globalism.
	Corporate Moral Agency	Concerned with the nature, liability, and responsibility of a corporation.
	Employee Rights	Concerned with the nature and types of rights that employees have. What do managers and corporations owe employees?
	Business and Environmental Ethics	Concerned with what responsibilities a business may have for the environment.
	Business Ethics and Religion	Concerned with what business practices may conflict with religious beliefs.
	Business Ethics and Social Responsibility	Concerned with what responsibilities a business may have for society at large.

Chart 55

Bioethics

Bioethics can employ any one of the different ethical theories explained in this chapter. See also chart 78.

Issues in Bioethics	**Faith and Bioethics**	Concerned with how one's faith determines what is right or wrong.
	Bioethics and the Law	Explores the relationship between what is legal and what is moral.
Ethical Issues in Health Care	**Truth Telling**	Should information ever be kept from a patient?
	Confidentiality	When should information about a patient be available to others?
	Consent Issues	**Competency**—What determines if a patient is competent to decide what sort of medical treatment he or she should or should not receive?
		Parents and Children—When is parental consent needed for children to receive medical treatment?
Life and Death Issues	**Abortion**	Concerned with terminating life before birth.
	Euthanasia	Concerned with terminating life before all medical treatments have been exhausted.
	Personhood	What constitutes a person? The key issue in life and death questions.
Reproduction	**In Vitro Fertilization**	Fertilization of the egg outside of the womb before implanting it.
	Cloning	Reproducing exact copies of living things by removing the DNA nucleus.
	Surrogacy	When one woman bears a child for another by in vitro fertilization.
Organ Donation	**Donations**	Concerned with the process of obtaining organs for transplants and determining how they should be used.
	Transplants	Concerned with the moral implications of moving organs from one person to another.
Genetics	**Gene Therapy**	The technology of treating ailments by manipulating one's genes.
	The Human Genome Project	The mapping of the set of genes found in every human.
	Genetic Screening	Using information from the human genome project to analyze a person's genetic makeup and detect future ailments and problems.
Experimentation	**Human**	Concerned with when and why experimentation on humans should be allowed.
	Animal	Concerned with when and why experimentation on animals should be allowed.

Chart 56

BIBLICAL FOUNDATIONS OF CHRISTIAN ETHICS

Hermeneutics

Biblical Hermeneutics: Assumptions

Premodern Assumptions *Hermeneutic of Trust* *Correspondence Theory of Truth*	**The Author of the Bible**	**Divine**—The author of the Bible is God.
		Human—God uses human instruments to communicate his truth.
	The Reader	Believes in miracles and the supernatural.
	Dominant Method of Interpretation	**Historical-Grammatical Interpretation**—An attempt to understand what the human author wrote.
		Allegory—Meanings the human author did not intend.
Modern Assumptions *Hermeneutic of Doubt* *Coherence Theory of Truth*	**The Author of the Bible**	Human authorship is assumed; there is no room for supernatural authorship.
	The Reader	Employs an antisupernatural bias because science can explain everything.
	Dominant Method of Interpretation	**Historical-Critical Methodologies**—Assume that the history of the Bible is unreliable. It attempts to interpret the Bible from a scientific standpoint.
Postmodern Assumptions *Hermeneutic of Suspicion* *Pragmatic Theory of Truth*	**The Author of the Bible**	Human authorship is assumed, but the possibility of supernatural authorship is not denied.
	The Reader	Does not believe that science can provide the answers. Allows for the possibility of the supernatural.
	Dominant Method of Interpretation	**Socio-Critical Methodologies**—An interpretative method based on the power of the interpretive community. It asserts that truth is what is good for the community.

Chart 57

Premodern Hermeneutics: Old Testament

Premodern Assumptions	**Authorship**	The Torah is divinely inspired. Hence, God is the author of the Torah.
	Correspondence Theory of Truth	Truth is what corresponds to reality. The Torah describes reality. The Torah contains the entire truth of God.
	Hermeneutic of Trust	Because of its divine inspiration, the Torah can be trusted.
		Inerrancy—The Torah is true without any admixture of error.
		Authority—The Torah has authority over every area of life.
		Sufficiency—The purpose of interpreting the Torah is to gain instruction for our lives. Nothing else is needed.
Method of Interpretation	**Categories of Hebrew Interpretation**	**Peshat**—Literal exegesis comparable to the historical-grammatical method of interpretation.
		Allegory—Extended metaphor. Meanings the human author did not intend.
		Midrash—Commentary or explanation of the Bible bounded by the community and its traditions.
		Pesher—Eschatological fulfillment in the contemporary situation.
	Apostolic Exegesis	**Typology**—Using ideas in the Old Testament as types that are found in the New Testament.
		Historicizing—Viewing the text in terms of prophecy and fulfillment.
		Reorientation—Finding Christ in the Old Testament.

Chart 58

Premodern Biblical Hermeneutics: Assumptions

According to Augustine in *De Doctrina Christiana* (*Christian Doctrine*), Augustine believed Christians must interpret the Bible in a way that is consistent with their faith. He also believed the Holy Spirit is needed to interpret the Bible.

Ethic of Interpretation *The right way to interpret the Bible is in accordance with the traditional faith of the Christian community. The reader must depend on the Holy Spirit for illumination.*	**Authorship**	There are two authors of the Bible. The first author is divine, the second is human. Thus the Bible is inspired (God-breathed). Interpretative methods must take both of these into account.
	Correspondence Theory of Truth	Truth is what corresponds to reality. The Bible describes reality.
	Hermeneutic of Trust	Because of its divine author, the reader can trust in the truth of the Bible.
		Inerrancy—The Bible is true without any mixture of error.
		Authority—Because of its divine author, the Bible provides guidance to the church.
		Sufficiency—Because of its divine author, believers do not need anything else as a guide for faith and practice.
Method of Interpretation *The Holy Spirit illumines the word of God.*	**1st Level of Interpretation**	**Historical-grammatical method** is used to obtain the human author's intent. This allows for the use of **lower-critical methodologies** such as textual criticism, form criticism, and rhetorical criticism.
	2nd Level of Interpretation	**Allegory** is used to obtain meanings the human author did not intend.
Limits on Interpretation *Only those within the Christian community can give valid interpretations of the Bible.*	**Creeds** *Only those who subscribe to the creeds are within the community.*	**Nicea** explains the deity of both the Father and the Son.
		Constantinople explains the deity of the Father, the Son, and the Holy Spirit.
		Chalcedon explains the nature of Christ.
	Theological Virtues *Are given by the Holy Spirit to guide and empower the Christian.*	**Love**—Valid interpretations are consistent with the love of God and the love of man for God's sake.
		Faith—Valid interpretations are consistent with Christian faith.
		Hope—Valid interpretations are consistent with Christian hope.

Chart 59

Modern Biblical Hermeneutics: Assumptions and Method

Ethic of Interpretation *The only right way to interpret the Bible is in a way that one (the individual) can be absolutely sure of the truth of the interpretation. This means in accordance with scientific principles.*	**Authorship**	The Bible has human authors only. Consequently, there is no room for the supernatural.
	Coherence Theory of Truth	Truth results from a coherent set of beliefs without contradiction. The Bible does not describe reality.
	Hermeneutic of Doubt	The Bible cannot be trusted for accuracy of any kind. The meaning of the text can be arrived at by scientific means.
		Inerrancy is rejected because: 1. inerrancy is a philosophical concept that is alien to the Bible 2. we do not have the original manuscripts 3. the Bible does not claim to be inerrant 4. an inerrant Bible requires an inerrant hermeneutic Modernists may sometimes argue for limited inerrancy, meaning that the Bible is inerrant in matters of faith and practice but not for issues of science or history. This is also called **infallibility**.
		Authority—The Bible has less authority than science and human reason.
		Sufficiency—The Bible must be supplemented by science to meet the needs of people.
Method of Interpretation *Scientific approaches are employed to interpretation, suggesting that the Bible must be interpreted like any other book. These approaches have an inherent antisupernatural bias.*	**Historical-Critical Method** *Developed by Baruch Spinoza in his* Political Theological Treatise. *Further developed by F. D. E. Schleiermacher (the father of modern hermeneutics and classical liberalism).*	*Higher criticism* is an approach to biblical interpretation that questions the Bible's veracity. It attempts to use "scientific methods" to understand the Bible. • **Source criticism**—Assumes that the authorship of each book is in question and seeks to find the original sources of the text. • **Form criticism**—Assumes that the form of the text was influenced by the style and form of other cultures. • **Redaction criticism**—Attempts to find what was added by others after the text was first written.
		Lower criticism is an attempt to look critically at the text without questioning the veracity of the Bible. • **Textual criticism**—Seeks to catalog and analyze textual variations to determine which text is the best. • **Rhetorical criticism**—Examines the structure of the text. Rhetoric helps find the primary meaning of the human author and shows the unity of a text.

Chart 60

Postmodern Biblical Hermeneutics

Ethic of Interpretation *The only right way to interpret the Bible is in a way that is advantageous to one's community.*	Authorship	The Bible has a human author.
	Pragmatic Theory of Truth	Truth is what works or is useful. The community determines what is true based on what is good for them. The Bible may or may not be useful, depending on which community one may be in.
	Hermeneutic of Suspicion	The reader operates with the belief that the writer is attempting to force his values on the reader.
		Inerrancy—If your community agrees that the text is inerrant, then the text is inerrant.
		Authority—The only authority the Bible has is what an individual or a community may give to it.
		Sufficiency—The sufficiency of the Bible is dependent on one's community.
Method of Interpretation *All of these approaches to the Bible employ a neo-Nietzchean will to power over the Scripture. Meaning does not reside with the text or with the author.*	**Socio-Critical Methods** *These are approaches to interpretation that are based in a community. They assert that knowledge is determined by a community.*	*Liberation theology* asserts that only the poor are capable of understanding the Bible. The wealthy are incapable of coming to a knowledge of the truth. The right interpretation is one that benefits the poor. Gustavo Gutierez is a leader in this hermeneutical/ethical method.
		Feminist theology asserts that only women are capable of understanding the Bible. A correct interpretation is one that benefits women. Rosemary Radford Ruether is a leader in this hermeneutical/ethical method.
		Black theology asserts that only black people can understand the Bible. A correct interpretation is one that benefits black people. James Cone is a leader in this hermeneutical/ethical method.
	Narrative Criticism	Asserts that truth is best communicated through the use of narrative.
	Reader Response	An approach to interpretation that asserts that meaning is determined by the reader.
	Structuralism	A movement led by Claude Lévi-Strauss, Roland Barthes, Jacques Lacan, and Michel Foucault, which replaced existentialism. Also known as **semiological analysis**.
	Poststructuralism	A movement away from structuralism led by Michel Foucault and Jacques Lacan.
	Deconstruction	A type of poststructuralism developed by Jacques Derrida. Takes advantage of the inherent instability of meaning in a text. It attempts to find novel and/or interesting meanings in a text. All of this is done for purposes of play.

Chart 61

Key Words for Biblical Ethics

Good	*Tov* (Heb.)	A state or function appropriate to genre, purpose, or situation; beautiful. Linked to personal faith in God.
	Agathos (Gk.)	Useful, morally good in relation to God, who is perfect (Matthew 19:17; Mark 10:17; Luke 18:18).
	Kalos (Gk.)	Beautiful, fine, free from defect, noble, or praiseworthy.
Righteous/Just	*Saddiq* (Heb.)	Righteous, just, lawful.
	Saddiqa (Heb.)	Righteousness, righteous acts.
	Dikaios (Gk.)	Upright, just, righteous. The righteous person fulfills his or her obligations to God and others.
Righteousness/ Justification	*Saddiq* (Heb.)	Do justice, declare righteous, make right.
	Dikaiosuna (Gk.)	Justice, uprightness.
Holy	*Qadosh* (Heb.)	Sacred, to be set apart, to belong to the sanctuary, dedicated for use by God.
	Hagios (Gk.)	Sacred, set apart for worship. There is an ethical aspect to *hagios* that includes a duty to worship and righteous living.
Sanctification	*Qadosh* (Heb.)	Be holy, consecrate.
	Hagiasmos (Gk.)	Holiness, consecration, sanctification.
Evil	*Awen* (Heb.)	Evil, iniquity, mischief, calamity.
	Raah (Heb.)	To be bad, displeasing. To be evil, to harm or bring calamity.
	Kakos (Gk.)	Evil, bad, wicked. *Kakos* and *poneros* are synonyms.
	Poneros (Gk.)	

Chart 62

Presuppositions of Christian Biblical Ethics

Moral Judgments	**Are Metaphysical Statements**	Moral judgments describe the will and nature of God. Moral judgments are statements about what is real.
	Are Universal	God's laws apply to all people everywhere at all times.
God	**Creator**	God is the creator of all that exists.
	Legislator	God determines right and wrong. He has ordered creation to reflect moral truth. His laws give moral direction.
Creation	**The Created Order**	The created order reflects the will and nature of God. Righteousness is woven into the very fabric of reality.
	Fact and Value	There is no dichotomy between fact and value. Value is an inherent part of creation.
The Bible	**Authority**	The Bible has authority for all ethical decisions.
	Inerrancy	The Bible provides ethical knowledge without admixture of error.
	Sufficiency	The Bible is all one needs to gain moral knowledge and make decisions.
Man	**Image of God**	Humans are made after the image of God. Consequently, humans have the ability to reason. Humans are also moral and spiritual creatures.
	Cognitivism	Moral knowledge results from a cognitive process. Emotions are just another aspect of moral judgment.
	Inability	Sin causes a *lack of moral knowledge.*
		Sin causes a *lack of power* to do what is right.

Chart 63

Old Testament

The Old Testament and Creation Ethics

The Creator	Yahweh is the creator of everything that exists. He created everything in accordance with his purposes. Righteousness is a key aspect of God's nature.		
	Justice	In the same semantic field as righteousness. Justice is established in the world order and is specified in the law of God. Every aspect of society is to reflect justice. The Israelite concept of justice relates to law, wisdom, nature, fertility, war, and victory over enemies.	
	Righteousness	Righteousness is also established in the world order. Thus God's nature is reflected throughout creation.	
		Acts of Salvation	*Acts of Salvation* Yahweh displayed his righteousness by his saving acts throughout the history of Israel. The prime example is the liberation of Israel in the exodus.
		Acts of Wrath	*Acts of Wrath* Yahweh also displayed his righteousness in acts of wrath. Those who act contrary to God's laws experienced his wrath. Thus Pharaoh perished when he tried to pursue the Israelites.
General Revelation	**Cosmic Order**	The cosmic order reflects God's nature and existence. Rather than chaos, this universe has order. There is purpose associated with this order. The world order has an axiological dimension that tells people how to live.	
	Seasonal Cycles	These cycles are part of the cosmic order. They are observed in the agrarian cycle and the four seasons. The regularity and stability of creation reflects the goodness of God. Since people depended on the agrarian cycle for food, they realized God supplied their needs.	
	Salvation History	God created and sustains the cosmic order just as he created and sustain history. This is not only the history of the world, but the history of Israel in particular. If the Israelites remained faithful to the covenant, God would bless them with the land.	
	New Creation	Creation is contingent upon God. As such, creation cannot be compared with God (Psalms 90:2; 102:25–27). God will create new heavens and a new earth (Isaiah 65:17; 66:22). The present creation is fallen and tainted by sin. Just as Israel will experience liberation in the eschaton, the old created order will be replaced by a new one.	
Special Revelation	**The Old Testament**	The Old Testament teaches a virtue ethic. It reflects the same truth found in general revelation. Over two-thirds of the Old Testament is in the form of narrative. Narrative is a key to learning virtue.	
		Law—These books emphasize the virtue of temperance or self-control. Obedience to the law requires self-control.	
		History—These books emphasize the virtue of courage. Courage was required to take possession of the land. Courage was also needed for one to remain faithful to God.	
		Poetry—These books emphasize the moral and intellectual virtue of wisdom (Gk. *phronesis*—practical reason). The wisdom literature teaches one how to live a successful life. The poetry teaches one to trust God in and in spite of circumstances.	
		Prophecy—These books emphasize the virtue of justice. The prophets continually cry out for justice.	

Chart 64

Creation Ethics and Cosmic Order

Cosmic Order	The cosmic order reflects God's nature and existence. Rather than chaos, this universe has order. There is purpose associated with this order. The world order has an axiological dimension that tells people how to live.		
Justice and Righteousness	These are established in the world order. Justice is specified in the law of God. This includes natural law and the divine law (the Bible). Every aspect of society is to reflect justice. The Israelite concept of justice relates to the law, wisdom, nature, fertility, war, victory over enemies, the sacrificial cult system, and the kingdom.		
	The Individual The individual is to treat everyone decently and should fulfill his or her duties for the good of the community (Isaiah 58:2; Ezekiel 18:7–18).		
	The King The king must execute justice and righteousness on behalf of God. To the degree that he does so, the kingdom prospers. David established justice and righteousness during his reign (2 Samuel 8:15; 20:23–26). All of Judah's kings were called for this purpose (Jeremiah 22:3; Ezekiel 45:9). Most of Israel's kings were unfaithful and did not act justly.		
	The Kingdom Israel's mission (Genesis 18:19; Isaiah 5:7; Jeremiah 4:2; Amos 5:24; Micah 6:8). Because Israel's kings were corrupt, the kingdom became corrupt as well. They did not act righteously, so God removed them from the land.		
Jesus Christ	Jesus Christ is the eschatological King who will rule justly and act righteously (Isaiah 9:6–7; 11:1–5; Jeremiah 23:5; 33:15). All of creation waits for his return, when it will be set free from its slavery to corruption (Romans 8:19–22).		
	The Righteousness of Christ	**The Cross**—The righteousness of Jesus Christ is displayed in his atoning work on the cross. Human works are not capable of making people righteous. Because of the cross of Christ, people of faith receive the mercy and grace of God. The cross is an atoning work in which guilt is acknowledged and removed.	
		The Resurrection—The righteousness of Jesus Christ is also seen in the resurrection. Because Jesus yet lives, his atoning death on the cross extends to all people, before and after, who confess their sin and repent.	
The Church *The church is part of the new creation.*	**Inaugurated Eschatology**—The church is the aspect of the kingdom of God (or heaven) that is already in existence.		
	The Redeemed—The church is the community of those who live in accordance with justice and righteousness.		
The Millennial Kingdom *The kingdom is the other part of the new creation.*	**Inaugurated Eschatology**—The millennial kingdom of God (or heaven) is the prophesied aspect of the kingdom that is not yet in existence. When Christ returns he will rule this kingdom in justice and righteousness.		
	The Redeemed—These people will live in a kingdom where there is perfect justice and righteousness, because they will have a perfect king.		
Wrath	Wrath is in store for all those who do not repent. It is coming because people have perverted justice.		

Chart 65

Creation Ethics and the Ten Commandments

The Ten Commandments are concerned with creation ethics. All ten reflect the Creator and the created order. Because these commandments are tied to the Creator and the created order (metaphysics), Old Testament ethics are teleological. These laws apply to all people everywhere. The rest of the law is concerned only with Israel. The law attests to the righteousness of God (Romans 3:21–26). All disobedience to God's laws is the result of idolatry.

The Creator	**Commandments 1–4** recognize that God is not a part of creation and that he is unique. Only by obeying these commandments can people live in justice and righteousness.
	1. Do not worship any other gods.
	2. Do not make idols.
	3. Do not use the name of the Lord irreverently.
	4. Honor the Lord on the Sabbath.
The Created Order	**Commandments 5–10** reflect the created order. Justice and righteousness require that one does what is best for the family and society as a whole.
	5. Honor your father and mother.
	6. Do not murder.
	7. Do not commit adultery.
	8. Do not steal.
	9. Do not lie.
	10. Do not desire anything that belongs to your neighbor.

Chart 66

Ethics in Jewish Apocalyptic Thought

Hebrew apocalyptic encourages the believer to be faithful and to act in accordance with righteousness and justice.

Characteristics of Apocalyptic Literature	• In apocalyptic thought there are **two ages**. The present age is an age of darkness. The future age is an age of light. In between the two ages is a time of intense tribulation. This time of tribulation is followed by the coming of the Messiah, who will defeat all of Israel's enemies. He will also establish a kingdom of righteousness. • Apocalyptic is primarily **written**, in contrast to prophecy, which is largely spoken ("Thus saith the Lord"). • Apocalyptic has **pseudonymous authorship**. • Apocalyptic is **esoteric** (understood by a few). • Apocalyptic employs **symbolic** language. • Apocalyptic is a type of **wisdom literature**.
Form of Apocalyptic Literature	• Description of **evil times**, tribulation. • The **day of the Lord** arrives. • The wicked are **punished**. • The faithful are **rewarded**.
Moral Lessons	God will act at the right time, so we must be patient and wait on him.
	When the Lord comes, he will punish the wicked.
	The patience of the faithful will be rewarded.

Chart 67

New Testament

The New Testament and Creation Ethics

The Gospels	**The Creator**	Only God is good (*agathos*). Jesus Christ is the Creator (John 1:1–3).
	The Created Order	Jesus refers to the law in reference to the created order (Matthew 5:18). Justice and righteousness result from fulfilling the law. Jesus also refers to creation with respect to marriage and divorce (Matthew 19:3–12).
	Salvation History	Jesus Christ is the eschatological King. The "Sermon on the Mount" is his announcement of the kingdom (Matthew 5:1–8:1). The parables (Matthew 13) explain the nature of the kingdom. He explains what will happen when he comes in his fullness and the ethical significance of his coming (Matthew 24–25).
	New Creation	Only those who are members of the kingdom will have eternal life in the new creation. Those who are not members of the kingdom will have eternal life in hell.
The Pauline Letters	**The Creator**	Jesus Christ is the Creator, and he is above all things (Colossians 1:15–22). To act justly and rightly, one must imitate Christ (1 Corinthians 11:1–3).
	The Created Order	Paul explains that the created order points to the nature and existence of God (Romans 1:19–32). Consequently, all people are accountable to the law and no one is blameless. The household codes testify to God's created order (Ephesians 5:21–6:9; Colossians 3:18–4:1). Paul explains that the state was also established by God (Romans 13) for justice and righteousness. In like manner, the church has an order established by God (1 and 2 Timothy, Titus).
	Salvation History	Paul explains that Adam and Christ represent corporate personalities. Adam is the old man, while Christ is the new man (Romans 5:6–21). Paul also uses apocalyptic language extensively throughout his letters. The church is an eschatological community (Ephesians 2:11–22). The Holy Spirit empowers and leads believers to live justly and righteously (1 Corinthians 12–14, Galatians). Believers are saved from the power of darkness (Ephesians 6:10–18; Colossians 1:13–14; 2:8–23).
	New Creation	Even creation yearns to be free from the effects of sin (Romans 8:18–39). Believers are a new creation in Christ (2 Corinthians 5:17; Colossians 3:1–4:6).
Peter	**The Creator**	God is holy, so righteousness involves obeying and imitating him (1 Peter 1:14–16). God is a perfect judge (1 Peter 1:17).
	The Created Order	Peter employed the household codes (1 Peter 3:1–8).
	Salvation History	Jesus Christ is the fulfillment of prophecy (1 Peter 1:10–12).
	New Creation	Believers have a new life (1 Peter 1:23–25). Believers look forward to a new heaven and a new earth (2 Peter 3:13).
John	**The Creator**	Jesus Christ is one with God the Father (John 8:58–59). God is love (1 John 4:16). Justice and righteousness mean acting in accordance with God's love.
	The Created Order	The created order is fallen and leads people away from God (1 John 2:15–17).
	Salvation History	Jesus Christ will come and put an end to sin and bring the wrath of God. His second coming will punish the wicked and save the righteous.
	New Creation	The new creation is realized in Revelation 21–22. Humans have communion with God and access to the tree of life as they did at the beginning (Genesis 1–3). Only believers will have access to this new creation.

Chart 68

The Sermon on the Mount

Matthew intended to portray Jesus Christ like a second Moses.

Up the Mountain	5:1–2	Jesus Christ went up the mountain like Moses.
The Nature of the Kingdom's Citizens	5:3–16	The citizens of the kingdom are blessed (*makarios*, happiness coming from God). These citizens desire the righteousness of God and are persecuted for it. The citizens of the kingdom glorify God in their lives.
Ten Commandments for the Citizens of the Kingdom of God *The citizens of the kingdom fulfill the Law and the Prophets through Jesus Christ (Matthew 5:17–20; 7:7–12).*	5:21–26	Do not hate your brother.
	5:27–32	Do not commit adultery.
	5:33–37	Do not make vows at all.
	5:38–42	Do not resist an evil person.
	5:43–48	Love your enemies and pray for those who persecute you.
	6:1–18	Do not practice your righteousness before others to be noticed by them.
	6:19–24	Do not store up for yourselves treasure in heaven.
	6:25–34	Do not worry about tomorrow.
	7:1–5	Do not judge.
	7:6	Do not give what is holy to dogs.
Invitation into the Kingdom	7:13–28	Jesus Christ invites his hearers to enter into the kingdom of God. The way is difficult and narrow, and few can enter in. Many false prophets point people to the wrong road. Only those who do the will of God will enter in.
Down the Mountain	8:1	Jesus Christ came down the mountain like Moses.

Chart 69

Blessedness (Happiness and Well-Being)

The righteous are blessed.

Greek Philosophy *Socrates, Plato, Aristotle, and the Stoics*	*Eudaimonia* *(Greek)*	Happiness from self-effort. *Eudaimonia* results from exercising natural (cardinal) virtues. *Eudaimonia* is not available to everyone. Slaves and those of lower station in life cannot attain it. Only those who are born well can attain *eudaimonia*.
	Makarios *(Greek)*	*Makarios* (happiness from the gods) comes with *eudaimonia* (happiness from self-effort).
	Felicitas *(Latin)*	Happiness from self-effort. Synonymous with *eudaimonia*. Augustine, Aquinas, and others employed this term and used it as distinct from *beatitudo*.

Biblical Ethics	*Makarios* *(Greek)*	Happiness/well-being coming from God. Blessedness comes when the believer exercises the theological virtues. It begins in this life and carries the believer into eternity. *Makarios* is available to anyone who becomes a Christian.
	Beatitudo *(Latin)*	Happiness/well-being coming from God. Synonymous with *makarios*. Augustine, Aquinas, and others employed this term. They did not confuse it with *felicitas*.
	New Testament	• Only *makarios* (*beatitudo*) is found in the NT (see Matthew 5:3–11; Luke 6:20–22). • *Makarios* is not synonymous with *eudaimonia* (*felicitas*), which is never found in the New Testament.

Chart 70

Righteousness in Jesus Christ

Jesus Christ	The Cross	Without the cross, humans cannot be justified and experience forgiveness for their sins (Hebrews 9:22).
Believers become the righteousness of God because of Christ (2 Corinthians 5:21).	**Resurrection**	The righteousness of God is made manifest in the resurrection.
	Acts of Salvation	Believers are made righteous in Jesus Christ because their sins have been forgiven (Romans 4:6–8, 25).
	Acts of Wrath	Humankind's sinfulness is deserving of God's righteous wrath (Romans 1:18–32).
Theological Virtues		Humans cannot be righteous on their own. They need the alien righteousness of Jesus Christ. The theological virtues are gifts of the Holy Spirit, created in believers, that unite them to Christ. The theological virtues make them a part of the new creation. These virtues give them the knowledge and power to live in a way that glorifies God.

Theological Virtues	**Faith** People are justified by faith in the work of Jesus Christ (Romans 5:1–11; Galatians 3:6–9). Faith helps believers to perceive the present in light of their future hope (Hebrews 11:1).
	Hope The justified live in the hope of their eternal righteousness in Jesus Christ (Romans 8; Galatians 5:5; 1 Thessalonians 1:10). Hope moves the thoughts of the believer from the present and into the future.
	Love Faith and hope grow out of love. Love fulfills the law of God (Matthew 22:36–40; Galatians 5:22–23).

Inaugurated Eschatology	A view with regard to both the individual Christian and the kingdom of God (or heaven). The kingdom of God is already here (in the church) but not yet (when Christ comes for his millennial reign).	
	Already	Believers are already declared righteous because they are new creations in Jesus Christ (2 Corinthians 5:17).
	Not yet	The righteousness of believers is not yet. Their righteousness will be made complete in the future (Romans 7:14–25).
Justification	Justification is being made righteous. The justification of the believer results from faith in Jesus Christ. Jesus Christ is the believer's justification (1 Corinthians 1:30).	
Sanctification	Sanctification is the process of being made more like Christ. It begins with justification and ends with glorification. Jesus Christ is the believer's sanctification (1 Corinthians 1:30).	

Chart 71

Jesus Christ and the Jubilee

Sabbath Year	The land was allowed to rest every seventh (Sabbath) year. After the seventh Sabbath year, the jubilee was celebrated.	
The Jubilee	The jubilee occurred once every fifty years. It was Yahweh's way of insuring justice and righteousness (Leviticus 25:1–55).	
	Release	People sold into slavery were released to return to their families.
	Return of the Land	Land that was sold to other Israelites was returned to the original families.
	The Poor	The debts of the poor were canceled.
Jesus Christ	Jesus Christ fulfills the prophetic jubilee to establish justice and righteousness (Isaiah 61:1; Matthew 11:2–6; Luke 4:14–21; 7:18–23).	
	Release and forgiveness	The atoning work of Jesus Christ frees people from their sins and sets them free from the dehumanizing effect of social roles and stigmas (Matthew 18:23–35; Mark 2:1–12; Luke 7:36–50; 19:1–10).
	Healing	Jesus restored the sight of the blind, made the lame walk, cleansed the lepers, restored the hearing of the deaf, and raised the dead (Matthew 11:4–6). As a result of forgiveness of sin, people are healed of their guilt and shame. People experience blessedness (*makarios*, the happiness that comes from God).
	Forgiveness of Debts	In the Lord's Prayer sins are equated with debts. Jesus Christ forgives people of both (Matthew 6:12–15; Mark 11:25–26; Luke 11:4).
	The Poor	Jesus proclaimed good news to the poor (Matthew 11:5; Luke 4:18). Blessed are the poor, those who mourn, and those who hunger and thirst for righteousness (Matthew 5:3–6; Luke 6:20–22).
	God as Sovereign	God sent Jesus Christ to proclaim the good news to the poor (Luke 4:18). This is the royal decree of liberty. God as king forgives people of their debts and punishes those who do not forgive their brothers and sisters (Matthew 18:21–35).

Chart 72

Part 3: Christian Beliefs

THEOLOGICAL FOUNDATIONS OF CHRISTIAN ETHICS

God

Doctrine of God

The Attributes of God	**Omnipotence**	God is perfectly powerful, which means he can do anything he purposes to do or anything that is consistent with his nature. Some argue that omnipotence entails the other attributes. God has the maximal set of powers that are coherent and consistent among themselves.
	Omniscience	God has perfect knowledge. He knows anything that can be known.
	Omnipresence	There is no place from which God is spatially or temporally distant.
	Omnibenevolence *God is perfectly good. God is the source and standard of good. He has at least six different moral attributes.*	**Holiness**—God is unique and set apart from all creation. He is also separate from sin and anything unclean.
		Righteousness/Justice—God always does right and what ought to be done. He acts in conformity to his nature and hence his law. God's law reflects the peace and order of his nature. God's own glory is the supreme objective.
		Love—God gives of himself to others.
		Mercy—God does not give us the punishment we deserve.
		Grace—God gives us unmerited favor. He gives what we do not and cannot earn.
		Patience—God withholds his judgment, giving people the opportunity to repent.
	Necessity	God necessarily exists in any possible world. If we understand goodness and beauty as aspects of being, then God is the personification of goodness and beauty.
Implications *The believer can trust God because he is perfectly good. God's word is trustworthy, and God will always do what is good and best.*	**Theodicy, the Problem of Pain, Evil, and Suffering**	Argues that if God has all of these attributes, then why does evil exist? Theodicy did not become a problem until the modern period, with its hermeneutic of doubt. During the premodern period, Augustine and others argued that God allows evil to exist because it serves his purposes.
	Impeccability	Teaches that God cannot sin. There are only two reasons why people sin. Either they lack wisdom/knowledge, or they lack power. If God is omnipotent and omniscient, he does not lack knowledge or power. Consequently, God cannot sin.
	Moral Realism	Moral facts depend on the existence of God.

Chart 73

Doctrine of God: The Creeds

Christian ethics requires not only moral action, but also belief in the right doctrines concerning who God is. It is only with the right understanding of who God is that one can live according to God's will. God's will is consistent with his nature.

Nicea *The council of **Nicea** in AD 325 decided that God is a Trinity. That is, the Father and the Son are coequal and share one substance. This doctrine was revised at the council of **Constantinople** in 381 to include the Holy Spirit.*	**Three Persons**	**Father**—Coequal and eternal with the Son and the Holy Spirit.
		Son—Jesus Christ, the God-man, is eternal and coequal with God the Father.
		Holy Spirit—The life-giver is eternal and coequal with God the Father. He proceeds from the Father.
	One Substance	All three persons share the same substance.
	Economic Trinity	The idea that the members of the Trinity have different functions.
	Perichoresis	The internal communication that goes on between the members of the Trinity.
	Errors	**Modalism**—There are not three separate persons in the Trinity. There is only one person who wears different "masks" at different times.
		Tritheism—The three persons are three separate Gods.
Chalcedon *In AD 451 the council of **Chalcedon** declared that Jesus Christ is one person with two natures.*	**One Person**	Jesus Christ, the Son, is the image of God.
	Two Natures	One nature is fully divine.
		One nature is fully human.
	Errors	**Arianism**—Suggests that the Son is a created being and not God.
		Subordinationism—Affirms that the Son is not created and that the Son is eternal. But denies that the Son is equal to the Father in his substance and attributes.
		Adoptionism—Suggests that God the Father adopted Jesus as his Son at his baptism. With this adoption, the Father bestowed supernatural powers upon the Son.

Chart 74

Creation

Creation

The Created Order	**Man**	Created after the image of God. Man has both rationality and senses. He was commanded to subdue the earth and all that is in it. He was also commanded to be fruitful and multiply.
	Woman	Created after the image of God as a helper of the man. She was created from the rib of the man to prevent him from being lonely. She was also made to help man fulfill God's command to be fruitful and multiply.
	Animals	Creatures made to fill the land, water, and sky.
Angelic powers *Angel (angelos) means messenger. Angels are created beings who have moral judgment, power, intelligence, and free will. They do not have bodies.*	**Archangels**	A higher order of angels. It is not clear whether there is only one (Michael) or more angels in this class (in Daniel 10:13 Michael is referred to as one of the chief princes).
	Angels over Humans	Organized as angels, authorities, powers, dominions, thrones, etc. (Colossians 1:13–16; 2:10–18). They can be over children (Matthew 18:10), nations (Deuteronomy 32:8; Daniel 10:13), the state (Romans 13:1, "authorities," *exousiai*), or the church (Revelation 1–3).
	Angels over Creation	The *stoicheia* are evil elemental powers or cosmic spirit powers that govern the physical elements, including the sun, moon, and stars (Colossians 2:8–20; Galatians 4:3–9). The *stoicheia* are personalized spiritual forces that have influence over many aspects of daily affairs.
The Fall *A rebellion against the created order. Genesis 3:1 begins with the serpent, moves to the woman, and finally to the man.*	**Creation**	The created order suffered damage in the fall. Because of sin, the world is not the way that it is supposed to be. Death and disorder (*akosmia*) reign. While it still points to God, the fallen world system leads people away from the truth.
	Angels	In the fall some angels rebelled. These angels are hostile to humans and their redemption. They seek to keep people blind and enslaved in sin. Fallen angels deceive people and keep them confused. They attack believers and ministers of the gospel. These fallen angels use social structures and other forms of control to prevent the spread of the gospel.
	Humans	In the fall the image of God was damaged. Thus, people's wills and affections are confused. Instead of loving God above all else, people love other things of far less value. The effects of the fall are not only affective, they are cognitive as well.

Chart 75

Augustine's Hierarchy of Thought

In *De Vera Religione* (*On True Religion*) Augustine equated goodness and beauty with being.

Ultimate Reality **(Truth)** ↑	**<u>Worship of God (the Creator)</u>** • *God* is eternal. As a necessary being, God is the most real of all things. God is the most beautiful and is the highest good. • *Fallen humans* can know some things about God through general revelation, but they cannot come to a full knowledge of who God is. God is above humankind's sensory perception, so our knowledge of him is limited. • *Believers* should love God above all else. God can only be fully revealed in his Word. Those who desire to know God must read his word, praise him, and pray to him.
True ↑	**<u>Thinking of Creation (the Real World)</u>** • All of *creation* reflects the nature of its Creator. As such, this world and everything in it is contingent. Everything that God created is good, but it is not eternal like God. • *Fallen humans'* sensory perception appreciates creation and is pointed to the Creator. Unfortunately, fallen humans often confuse creation with the Creator. Fallen humans love what is true rather than what is truth. • *Believers* also perceive the creation, but they remember that it is only temporal and should not be loved more than the Creator.
Falsehood	**<u>Vice (Fiction—a Mixture of the Real World and Falsehood)</u>** • *Vice* results from an improper love of creation. • *Fallen humans* participate in creation by satisfying their lusts, such as eating, drinking, and engaging in sexual intercourse. They use their minds for that which is not fruitful because their view of creation is corrupt, and they worship idols. • *Believers* should avoid this state of mind.
↑ **Ultimate Unreality** **(Fantasy)**	**<u>Fantasy (Amusement)</u>** • *Fantasy* is the least real of all things because it is based on imagination. This is the worst state of affairs. • *Fallen humans* spend most of their free time fantasizing. Their view of creation is corrupt, and they cannot free themselves from these views. Consequently, fallen humans cannot be happy. • *Believers* should spend little or no time fantasizing.

Chart 76

Man

Doctrine of Man

Man's nature plays a major role in the understanding of Christian ethics.

The Image of God	**Personality**	Man has an individual nature. The individual personality extends through everything he owns. When one gives a gift, he gives part of himself.
	Spirituality	Man is a spiritual creature made to glorify God.
	Rationality	Man can reason to a degree far higher than any animal.
	Morality	Man is a creature designed to do God's will.
	Authority	Man is a creature whom God has given authority over the earth.
	Creativity	Man is a creature who can improvise and re-create.
Psychosomatic Unity *The body and the spirit are so intertwined as to be inseparable except at death.*	**Body**	**Body**—The physical aspect of man.
		Sarx—The part of man in which sin dwells.
	Spirit	**Spirit**—*Pnuema*, the mental aspect of man.
	Soul	**Soul**—The union of the spirit to the body (Genesis 2:7).
	Dichotomy	Man has two components, the body and the spirit.
Man's Social Nature	**Corporate Personality**	Man is a social creature. He has a nature that makes him part of a group. The leader of that group is the **corporate head.** **Representation** is when the corporate head represents the group. The group can be a family, a city, or a nation.
	Corporate Responsibility	The corporate head of a group can take actions that result in praise or blame for that group. **Corporate blessing** can extend to one's descendants for many generations. In like manner, **corporate cursing** can extend to one's descendants.
	Oscillation	Man's personality oscillates between his individual and corporate natures (see Genesis 1:27; Joshua 7:24–26; 2 Samuel 1–9).
	Realism	These ideas have their basis in metaphysics (ontology). The essence of a thing determines what it is. Just as an acorn is a potential tree, a man (as a social animal) is a potential community. This is why the community should come before the individual, and duties to the community should come before the rights of the individual.

Chart 77

Implications of the Image of God: Issues of Life and Death

Abortion (*Termination of a pregnancy*)

Types of Abortion	Spontaneous abortion—Generally referred to as a miscarriage.
	Human intervention abortion—What is generally thought of as an abortion.
Factors in Abortion	The ontological status of the fetus—Concerned with the nature of the fetus. Is it, or is it not a person? If it is a person, then abortion is wrong. If it is not a person, then abortion is permissible.
	The moral status of the fetus—Concerned with whether the fetus has rights. Liberals believe that the moral status of the fetus is contingent upon the ontological status of the fetus. Conservatives believe that because the fetus is in the image of God, it inherently has rights.
	The health of the mother—Is the safety of the mother at risk? Does this have any bearing on the morality of abortion?
	The rights of the mother—Those in favor of abortion argue that abortion is only concerned with the rights of the mother.
	The beginning of life—Those against abortion argue that life begins at conception. Those for abortion argue that life begins at birth.

Christians believe that voluntary abortion is wrong because the fetus is a person made after the image of God. Christians generally believe that life begins at conception. Christians dispute whether or not the safety of the mother is a factor in abortion.

Euthanasia (*Lit. "good death"—the termination of life for convenience*)

Types of Euthanasia	Active euthanasia—The deliberate (voluntary) termination of human life.
	Passive euthanasia—Allowing one to die from natural causes.
Factors in Euthanasia	Personhood—Concerned with determining whether or not the patient is a person.
	Death—What constitutes death? Some suggest total cessation of respiration and blood flow. Others suggest cessation of brain activity.

Christians believe that *active euthanasia* is wrong because the patient is always a person made after the image of God.

Life and Death Issues

Both abortion and euthanasia are concerned with personhood.

Christians believe that because humans are made after the image of God, human life should not be treated lightly; to do so is murder.

These ideas imply that human beings should not be treated as things.

Consequently, issues like cloning and experimentation with human embryos is wrong.

Chart 78

Views of the Conscience

There are a number of views concerning how moral knowledge is gained.

Aristotle	**Prudence** *A special virtue*	Prudence is a **moral virtue** used to determine right and wrong.
		Prudence is an **intellectual virtue** used for wisdom.
The Old Testament	**Heart** *(leb)*	There is no Hebrew word for "conscience." Moral knowledge is determined in the heart.
The New Testament	**Synoida** *(syneidesis)*	The Jews understood the conscience to be a faculty used for moral judgment. Paul uses this word group extensively (1 Corinthians 4:4; 8:7–12; 10:25–29; 2 Corinthians 1:12; 4:2; 5:11; Romans 2:15; 9:1; 13:5).
Medieval	**Peter Lombard** *Wrote* The Sentences. *The conscience has two major components.*	*Synderesis* is the Latin transliteration for the Greek word *syneidesis*. It is an innate disposition that connects moral knowledge to the will.
		Conscientia is the Latin word for the virtue prudence or practical wisdom. It derives from the Greek word *syneidesis*—"with" (*syn/con*) and "knowledge" (*oida / scio*).
	Thomas Aquinas	*Synderesis* is a disposition that cannot err in moral judgment.
		Conscientia can err in moral judgment. *Conscientia* only draws conclusions from principles grasped by *synderesis*.
	Bonaventure	*Synderesis* takes information from *conscientia* and uses it to move the will.
		Conscientia is the natural law written in our hearts.
British Empiricists	**Cambridge Platonists** *Clergymen who studied at Cambridge*	Benjamin Whichcote (1609–83), John Smith (1616–52), Ralph Cudworth (1617–88), Nathaniel Culverwel (1618–51), and Peter Sterry (1613–72). They believed that moral knowledge was gained through a moral sense and the reading of Scripture.
	3rd Earl of Shaftesbury	Student of John Locke who believed that moral knowledge resulted from a moral sense.
	Francis Hutcheson	Systematized Shaftesbury's ideas. Believed that there is a moral and aesthetic sense (called taste).
	Bishop Joseph Butler	Contemporary of Hutcheson. He believed that human nature is complex but normative. Human nature is ruled by the voice of God within us. He rejects moral sense theory and *synderesis* but believes in an inerrant conscience.
	Sentimentalists *Students of Francis Hutcheson*	David Hume believed that the moral sense is nothing more than the passions.
		Adam Smith believed that the moral sense is nothing more than the passions.

Chart 79

Eschatology (Three Views)

The study of last things. The kingdom of God is an important feature of the New Testament.

Consistent Eschatology *Developed by Albert Schweitzer*	• The kingdom is **yet future**. • Christian ethics are only an interim ethic of obedience to God's will.
Realized Eschatology *Developed by C. H. Dodd*	• The kingdom is **here in the church**. • Christian ethics involves eschatology, a new age of God's working power. • It also involves the "body of Christ" because it is a social ethic. • The imitation of Christ is essential to Christian ethics. While it involves the social virtues, love is primary.
Inaugurated Eschatology *Developed by Oscar Cullmann and then by George Eldon Ladd*	• It combines consistent eschatology with realized eschatology. • The kingdom is **already but not yet**. • The kingdom is present in the church but has yet to be fulfilled. • The kingdom will be completely fulfilled with the second coming of Christ. • Christian ethics are an example of the future breaking into the present. • The New Testament ethic is an ethic of redemptive history because it is concerned with fulfilling the Old Testament. • Believers must be radically obedient to the divine will at every moment. • Believers must follow the leading of the Holy Spirit. • No area of human existence is excluded from moral judgment, because the lordship of Christ involves all things.

Chart 80

Soteriology

Soteriology is intertwined with **eschatology**, **anthropology**, and **Christology**.

Anthropology	**The Doctrine of Man**	All humans are in the corporate personality of **Adam** or of **Christ** (Romans 5:6–21).
	Adam	• Those in the corporate personality of Adam die. • In Adam all people are slaves to sin.
	Christ	• Those who are part of the corporate personality of Christ are made righteous. • In Christ people have knowledge and power over sin.
Christology	**Son of Man**	Jesus referred to himself as the Son of Man, a title found in Daniel 7. In this passage the multitude of the righteous are represented by the Son of Man.
	Son of God	Jesus is also the Son of God, so he is fully divine.
	The Second Adam	Jesus is the second Adam because of his sinless obedience to the Father.
	Virgin Birth	Because he was born of a virgin, Jesus was not tainted by the effects of Adam's sin.
	Messiah	Jesus is the promised "anointed one." He reigns in heaven with God the Father, and he will reign on earth from Israel as well.
	Savior	Because of his perfect, sinless life and his atoning death on the cross, Jesus Christ is the Savior of all who believe in him.
Eschatology	**Inaugurated Eschatology** *The kingdom is already but not yet.*	Paul uses the corporate examples of **Adam** and **Christ** as a major feature in his interpretation of Old Testament texts. He uses this typology in his discussion of the "old man and the new man" (Romans 6:6; Ephesians 2:15; 4:22). Paul also uses it with his explanation of the inner man and the outer man (Romans 7:22; 2 Corinthians 4:16). Last, Paul uses these ideas to explain the difference between the carnal man and the spiritual man (Romans 8:8).
	Already	Because believers are in Christ, they experience his power to live righteously. Unfortunately, believers are still part of the corporate personality of Adam, so Christians still sin.
	Not Yet	Believers still struggle with sin, but they will be glorified and triumph over it in the future.

Chart 81

Divinization

Justification *The first step in the individual's redemption.*	Concerned with imparting the righteousness of God in the believer. Justification happens with regeneration.	
	Theological Virtues *These are created in the believer by the Holy Spirit to empower the believer for a righteous life. There are three of these.*	**Beatitude**—The happiness that comes from God when one exercises the theological virtues.
		Love—The love of God and the love of others for God's sake. Faith and hope grow out of love. To act out of love is to fulfill the commandments.
		Faith—Humans are justified by faith. Faith is the gift of God.
		Hope—Believers live in hope of the future life in Christ.
Sanctification *Sanctification does not happen without justification.*	**Impartation of Holiness**	The first aspect of holiness is to be set apart. Believers are to be in the world but not part of it.
		The second aspect of holiness is to grow in moral goodness. Believers should become more Christlike as time goes on.
	Three Stages	**Stage 1** of sanctification begins at regeneration.
		Stage 2 of sanctification continues throughout the life of the believer.
		Stage 3 of sanctification concerns its completion. Some argue that sanctification is completed at the death of the believer or the return of Christ. Others argue that sanctification is not completed in this life.
	Involves Both God and Man	**God**—Because of the atoning work of Christ and believers' union with him, believers become more Christlike over time. The Holy Spirit gives Christians knowledge and power over sin.
		Man—People are still free and must decide to follow after Christ. Believers must still read Scripture and do what it says to grow in Christlikeness.
Glorification *Glorification does not happen without justification and sanctification.*	**The Final Step of Redemption**	• Moral and spiritual perfection. • The resurrection body. • Glorification will happen for some at the resurrection. • Glorification will happen for others at the return of Christ.

Chart 82

The Work of the Holy Spirit

Theological Virtues *These are given for the good of the individual believer.*	• **Love**—The love of God and the love of others for God's sake. It is the root of the other theological virtues. • **Faith**—Grows out of love and justifies believers. • **Hope**—Helps believers to focus on eternity and to live in light of it.
Beatitudes *Happiness that comes from God (Matthew 5:3–12). This results from exercising the theological virtues.*	• **The Poor in Spirit**—Those who realize their spiritual poverty are happy because they will find Jesus Christ. • **The Mourners**—Those who mourn over their spiritual poverty will be saved. • **The Meek**—Those who mourn over their spiritual poverty cannot be proud. They will live their lives in submission to Christ. • **The Merciful**—They are blessed because they have received mercy from God. Consequently, they are merciful to others. • **The Hungry**—The saved hunger and thirst for all the righteousness there is. • **The Pure in Heart**—These righteous ones are unmixed, unalloyed in their devotion to God. • **The Peacemakers**—The saved are blessed because they have made their peace with God. They also seek to spread this peace to others. • **The Persecuted**—The persecuted are happy because they are counted worthy to suffer for Christ.
Fruit of the Spirit *These are evidences that are manifested in the life of the believer.*	• **Love**—The love of God and the love of others for God's sake. It is the root of all spiritual fruit. • **Joy**—Believers are content regardless of circumstances. • **Peace**—Believers experience the peace of God. • **Longsuffering**—Believers hold on to Christ in spite of trials. • **Kindness**—Believers go out of their way to benefit others. • **Goodness**—Believers attempt to please God, not themselves. • **Faith**—Believers trust God's goodness and providence. • **Meekness**—Believers are not proud or arrogant. • **Self-Control**—Believers live a disciplined life.
Gifted People *These gifts are given for the edification of the church body.*	• **Apostles**—An office with the ability to start new churches. • **Prophets**—An office with the ability to speak for God. • **Teachers**—An office with the ability to effectively communicate the truth of God's Word. • **Evangelists**—An office with the ability to effectively communicate the gospel. • **Pastors**—An office with the ability to lead a congregation well. This includes the ability to teach and preach.
Spiritual Gifts	• **Administration**—The ability to wisely use the resources of the church. • **Helps**—The ability to do whatever needs to be done in the church. • **Mercy**—The ability to demonstrate love and concern for those in need or those in difficult circumstances. • **Miracles**—The ability to do supernatural acts to demonstrate the power of God. • **Healing**—The ability to heal the sick supernaturally. • **Tongues**—The ability to speak in a human language that one did not learn through natural means. • **Interpretation**—The ability to interpret the gift of tongues.

Chart 83

Spiritual Warfare

The Nature of the Fight	**The Fight against Sin**	Believers must fight against sin and temptation.
	The Fight for the Truth	Believers must earnestly contend for the faith once for all delivered to the saints (Jude 3). Teachers of false doctrine are numerous and must be confronted. The enemy employs speculations and lofty things to fight against the knowledge of God (2 Corinthians 10:5).
	The Fight to Spread the Gospel	Believers engage in spiritual warfare every time they attempt to share the gospel with the lost.
The Enemy *The primary enemy is Satan, but he is assisted by angelic powers of all orders.*	• **Rulers** • **Powers** • **World forces** • **Spiritual Powers of Wickedness** • *Stoicheia*	These are angelic powers that have charge over different parts of creation (Ephesians 6:10–18). These powers use social structures, among other means, to achieve their ends. They have taken part in the rebellion against God. Jesus Christ is superior to and has overcome these powers (Colossians 1:13–20; 2:15, 18–20).
The Armor of God *Ephesians 6:10–18*	**Belt of Truth**	A belt provides protection to the loins so that one can reproduce. Believers need to know and keep the truth if they are to reach others for Christ.
	Breastplate of Righteousness	Believers must live righteous lives if they are to have any success in doing the work of God. Living righteous lives offers believers great protection.
	Shoes of the Gospel of Peace	Believers must be ready at all times to give the gospel to others. Soldiers need good shoes if they are to march or advance in battle.
	Shield of Faith	Faith provides protection when the enemy is causing believers pain and difficulty. Believers can hide behind their shields of faith when the enemy throws fiery darts at them.
	Helmet of Salvation	Just as helmets protect soldiers from the death-dealing blows of the enemy, salvation protects believers from all of the vicissitudes involved in following Christ.
	Sword of the Spirit	The short sword (*makira*) requires skill for effective use. Believers must study the Word of God and hide it in their hearts if they are to use it effectively.
	Prayer	Believers must pray constantly and in accordance with the Word of God to stop the enemy from accomplishing his goals.

Chart 84

Marriage and Family

Purpose of Marriage	• God commanded man to be fruitful and multiply (Genesis 1:28). • It is not good for man to be alone (Genesis 2:18). • Man is made after the image of God, so man is a social creature. • According to Augustine, woman was created to help fulfill God's command to be fruitful and multiply.	
God's Design for Marriage	**Monogamy**	God's design for marriage is one man with one woman for a lifetime. Any sexual relations outside of marriage are wrong.
	Divorce	God allowed divorce because of the hardness of men's hearts (Matthew 19:8).
		Divorce is allowed for unrepentant adultery (Matthew 5:27–31; 19:9).
		Divorce is allowed if an unbelieving spouse deserts the believing one (1 Corinthians 7:12–16).
	Remarriage	Some believe that remarriage is allowed only when one's spouse is deceased.
		Others believe that remarriage is allowed only when divorce occurs for scriptural reasons.
		Still others believe that remarriage can occur whenever one is divorced.
	Homosexuality	Homosexuality is clearly outside of God's design (1 Corinthians 6:9). Effeminate (Gk. *arsenikos*—the female actor in a homosexual act). Homosexual (Gk. *molokos*—the male partner in the homosexual act).
The Family **Household Codes** *Ephesians 5:22–6:9; 1 Peter 3:1–7*	**Order**	**Egalitarians** emphasize the idea that men and women are equal to such an extent that men's and women's roles are interchangeable and that husbands and wives should submit to each other.
		Complementarians believe that men and women are equal but have different roles or functions. Consequently, they believe that the man is the leader in the household. They believe that the man is the head of the wife (Ephesians 5:23).
	Husbands	Husbands should love their wives just as Christ loved the church (Ephesians 5:25–29). Fathers should not provoke their children to anger (Ephesians 6:4).
	Wives	Wives should submit to their husbands as to the Lord (Ephesians 5:22–24).
	Children	Children should obey their parents because this is right (Ephesians 6:1–3).

Chart 85

Church

The Church

Purpose	**Glorify God**	While worship is a primary example of glorifying God, all that the church does should give glory to him.
	Teach	Teaching sound doctrine is an essential part of making disciples and is an important way to glorify God.
	Evangelize	God is glorified when people come to a saving knowledge of Jesus Christ.
Nature	**The Kingdom**	The church is the "already here" part of the kingdom of God (or heaven). The New Testament refers largely to the individual local church. The church is also universal and invisible.
	The Saved	The members of the church are all joined in Christ (corporate personality of Christ).
	The Lost	The church also has members who are not in Christ.
Structure	**Pastors**	The pastor (Gk. *poimen*, "shepherd") is responsible for the leading and the feeding of the sheep.
	Elders	The elders assist the pastor in his work of leading and feeding the sheep.
	Deacons	The deacons are servant leaders. They are not the equivalent of pastors or elders because they are not required to teach. They are gifted for roles of limited leadership in the church.
	Laity	Each believer is a priest who is gifted by the Holy Spirit to contribute to the needs of the congregation.
Church Discipline	**Purpose**	The purpose of church discipline is to bring a believer who is causing damage to the body of Christ to a place of repentance so that he or she may be restored to the church body without causing further damage.
	Immorality	Open immorality is a chief reason to exercise church discipline.
	Factions	Those who cause discord need to be disciplined.
	False Teaching	Those who teach false doctrine should also experience church discipline.

Chart 86

Types of Churches

Revelation 2–3 contains letters written to seven churches. While these were actual churches, they also represent seven types of churches. Each of these churches receives praise and condemnation. Each church is composed of both believers and unbelievers whose actions result in their praise or condemnation. Consequently, these churches serve as models to emulate and avoid.

Ephesus 2:1–7	*Positive*	This church is praised for their good deeds, perseverance, and hard work. They are also praised because they reject false teaching.
	Negative	They had left their first love, the love for Christ. Consequently, they did all the right things for all the wrong reasons.
Smyrna 2:8–11	*Positive*	They patiently endure tribulation. They are spiritually rich.
	Negative	None.
Pergamum 2:12–17	*Positive*	They hold fast to Christ's name and do not deny their faith.
	Negative	They have people teaching false doctrine and people involved in immorality. They also have those involved in idolatry.
Thyatira 2:18–29	*Positive*	They have good deeds, love, faith, service, and perseverance. The good deeds grow in number.
	Negative	They are led by a prophetess, Jezebel. They tolerate false teachers and commit acts of immorality. They are involved in idolatry.
Sardis 3:1–6	*Positive*	None.
	Negative	They are spiritually dead. Their deeds are not completed in the sight of God.
Philadelphia 3:7–13	*Positive*	They have good deeds. They have endured persecution. They have kept God's Word and have not denied the name of Christ.
	Negative	None.
Laodicea 3:14–22	*Positive*	None.
	Negative	Their deeds are neither hot nor cold. They are spiritually wretched, miserable, poor, blind, and naked.

Chart 87

State and Church

The State

Church and State	**The Church over the State**	From AD 312 until the Enlightenment in the seventeenth century, the church stood over the state. In many cases, the church abused its power.
	The Church with the State	This is an ideal situation that rarely exists for any period of time. The U.S. Constitution was written with this idea in mind. The church and the state are separate spheres of authority without power over each other.
	The State over the Church	This is the most common of situations. It may be accompanied by persecution of the church.
The State and the Sword	**Criminal Justice** *Romans 13:1–6;* *1 Peter 2:11–12*	• The state is given by God for the good of the people. • The state has the authority to establish and enforce laws. • The state has the authority to wage war. • The state has authority to execute capital punishment. • Christians should obey the law of the land until it prevents them from preaching the gospel.
	Just War	According to Augustine, a war is just only when • it is done with legitimate authority. • it is a last resort. • it is done to punish or prevent aggression. • it is motivated by love. • it is performed with mercy and restraint.
The State and Economics	**Coinage**	According to Matthew 17:24–27; 22:15–21; Mark 12:14–17; and Luke 20:22–26, Jesus affirmed the state's authority to make money and tax its citizens.
	Law and Monetary Policy	The Bible does not specify any economic system, although it is clear that Israel had a free-market economy. Israel's system included taxation and laws to take care of the poor.
	Taxation	Paul emphasized the state's authority to tax.

Chart 88

Christ and Culture

Based on *Christ and Culture* by H. Richard Niebuhr
This chart is modified with permission of Bill Goff.

	Description	Adherents	Strengths	Weakness
Christ against Culture	Christian ethics is concerned with living out the faith in a corrupt and fallen world.	Ascetics, Tertullian, Anabaptists, Quakers	Christians are separated from the sinful influence of the world.	Christians have no influence on the world.
Christ of Culture	Christian ethics is an example of the best value system the world can have.	Clement of Alexandria, classical liberals, Eastern Orthodox Church, social gospel, liberation theology	Christianity at least attempts to influence the world.	Christianity becomes devoid of faith in Jesus Christ.
Christ above Culture	Christian ethics are superior to the kinds of ethics revealed by general revelation.	Anselm, Abelard, Thomas Aquinas, Bonaventure, Duns Scotus	Relates Christian worldview to philosophy in general.	Can give too high a place to human reason.
Christ and Culture in Paradox	The world is fallen, but Christians are still called to live in it. They are also called to improve things as much as possible.	Martin Luther, Emil Brunner, Reinhold Niebuhr	The church has the favor of the society and the state. As such it can have significant influence.	The church can be tempted to compromise and settle for the status quo.
Christ the Transformer of Culture	Culture should be transformed in accordance to a Christian worldview.	Augustine, John Calvin, Moral Majority	The church has power over the state and can make great change.	The church may depend more on political power than on the power of God.

Chart 89

The Church and the World

The World *1 John 2:15–17*	**Literal Meaning**	System, order (Gk. *kosmos*).
	Nature of the World	A system of angelic powers in rebellion against its creator (Ephesians 2:2; 6:12). It is contrary to the will of God.
	Composition of the World	**Lust of the Flesh**—Things contrary to the will of God that attract the baser desires of people.
		Lust of the Eyes—things that are contrary to the will of God that attract.
		Boastful Pride of Life
	Duration of the World	The existence of the world is only temporary.
	The Lost	Those without Christ love the world. These people do not have the love of the Father.
	Christians	Christians who have friendship with the world are called adulterers (James 4:4). Believers should strive to be free of the love of the world. The cares of the world choke the Word of God so that believers become unfruitful (Matthew 13:22). The world hates believers because while they live in the world, they have no part of it (John 17:6–19).
The Church	**Literal Meaning**	Called-out ones (Gk. *ekklesia*).
	Nature of the Church	A present manifestation of the kingdom of God (or heaven).
	Purpose of the Church	The purpose of the church is to glorify God by calling all people to repentance so that they will live according to God's will.
	Composition of the Church	The kingdom is composed of both believers and unbelievers (Matthew 13:24–30, 36–43, 47–50).
	The Lost	At the end of time, the unbelievers will be separated from the believers and be cast into the fire.
	Christians	Christians do the will of God. Consequently, they will live forever (1 John 2:17).

Chart 90

Christian Decision Making

Christian decision making involves a number of important factors.

Divine Command	**The Will of God**	God's divine commands are consistent with his will.	
	The Nature of God	God's divine commands are also consistent with his nature.	
Revelation	**General Revelation**	God's divine commands are consistent with natural law.	
	Special Revelation	**Old Testament**	God's divine commands and natural law are consistent with the Old Testament.
		New Testament	God's divine command and natural law are consistent with the New Testament.
The Holy Spirit *Gives guidance and power to believers to live righteously.*	**Theological Virtues** *Believers decide in accordance with the theological virtues.*	**Love**	The love of God and the love of others for God's sake. Love fulfills the law of God.
		Faith	Faith grows out of love. We are justified (made righteous) by faith.
		Hope	Hope grows out of love and helps believers live rightly because they focus on eternity.
Community	**Anthropology**	Humans are social creatures, and their actions should be viewed from the perspective of a community.	
	Family	God established the family. The family is the basic building block of society. The right action is generally one that acts to the benefit of the family. The family interests should be followed until they conflict with the law of God.	
	State	God established the state. The state exists as an agent of God. Right action is generally within the laws of a state. The state should be obeyed until it conflicts with the law of God.	
	Church	God established the church. The church is the present manifestation of the kingdom of God (or heaven). For believers, right action is in accordance with God's Word, which never conflicts with the law of God.	
		Creeds and the *regula fidei* (Lat. *"rule of faith"*)	The creeds (Apostles', Nicene/Constantinopolitan, Chalcedonian) determine the boundaries for who is in the community of believers.

Chart 91

HISTORY
OF
ETHICS

Historical Overview

Overview of Philosophical Worldviews

Premodernism (Recorded history to 1600)	**Modernism** (1600–1950)	**Postmodernism** (Continental Philosophy) (1950–present)

METAPHYSICAL ISSUES

• Begins with metaphysical presuppositions. • Inherent belief in God and the supernatural. • Belief that God has ordered the world to reflect his nature. • Most subscribed to metaphysical realism. • Rules of logic apply.	• Status of God and the supernatural is questionable. • Metaphysics is reduced to ontology.	• Allowance is made for the supernatural. • Ontology is equated with hermeneutics.

EPISTEMOLOGICAL ISSUES

• The order of the world makes it understandable. • Knowledge is found in the community. • Special revelation is accepted along with reason. • Creeds and traditions (such as canons) are seen as legitimate sources of knowledge. • Correspondence theory of truth. • Hermeneutic of trust.	• Search for **Cartesian certainty** (absolute certainty of knowledge). • **Methodological doubt** (doubting everything that one cannot be certain of) used to attain Cartesian certainty. • Reason is emphasized; rejection of the supernatural, creeds, and tradition. • Science is the supreme kind of knowledge. • The rules of logic apply. • The individual is placed over the community. • **Epistemology** splits into two camps: the empiricists and the rationalists. • **British empiricists** allowed the use of both inductive and deductive logic. • **British empiricists** held to a correspondence theory of truth. • **Continental rationalists** used only deductive logic. They held a coherence theory of truth.	• Pragmatic theory of truth. • Hermeneutic of suspicion. • There are no facts, only interpretations. • Knowledge is found in the community because the community has power. • Science is incapable of delivering the truth. • Knowledge is gained by intuition and feeling. • Epistemology is reduced to hermeneutics. • Rules of logic do not apply.

AXIOLOGICAL ISSUES

• The order in the world reveals what is right and what is wrong. • Ethics and aesthetics are teleological. • Rights are subordinated to duties. • The individual is subordinated to the community.	• Ethics are about individual decisions. • **British empiricists** subscribed to utilitarianism. • Many, but not all, **British empiricists** subscribed to a moral sense theory. • **British empiricists** believed that ethics and aesthetics are closely related. • Aesthetic knowledge is delivered by a part of the moral sense called "taste." • **Continental rationalists'** premier ethical theories came from Immanuel Kant. • **Continental rationalists** separated ethics from aesthetics. • Many, but not all, **continental rationalists** believed that moral knowledge arrived via reason.	• Ethics are found in the community because the community has power. • Axiology is reduced to hermeneutics. • There is no objective morality.

Chart 92

Overview of Philosophers and Ethicists

Premodern		Modern	Postmodern
Classical Period **500 BC–AD 500**	*Medieval Period* **AD 500–1500**	**AD 1600–1900**	**1950–present**
Major Philosophers • Plato • Aristotle **Stoics** • Zeno • Cicero • Epictetus **Epicureans** • Epicurus **Major Theologians** • Augustine	**Major Theologians** • Bonaventure • Thomas Aquinas • John Duns Scotus • William Ockham • Francisco Suarez • Hugo Grotius • Martin Luther • John Calvin	**British Empiricists** • Thomas Hobbes • The Cambridge Platonists • John Locke • Anthony Ashley Cooper • Samuel Clark • Bernard de Mandeville • Francis Hutcheson • Joseph Butler • David Hume • Adam Smith • Jeremy Bentham • John Stuart Mill • Henry Sidgwick **Analytic Philosophers** • G. E. Moore • A. J. Ayer • W. D. Ross • R. M. Hare • J. L. Mackie • G. E. M. Anscombe • John Rawls • Martha Nussbaum • Philippa Foot • Alasdair MacIntyre **Continental Rationalists** • René Descartes • Nicolas de Malebranche • Baruch Spinoza • Jean Jacques Rousseau • G. W. Leibniz • Immanuel Kant **Continental Philosophers** • G. F. W. Hegel • Arthur Schopenhauer • Søren Kierkegaard • Friedrich Nietzsche • Martin Heidegger • Jean-Paul Sartre	**Contemporary Christian Ethicists** • Joesph Fletcher • Paul Ramsey • John H. Yoder • James Gustafson • Stanley Hauerwas • James McClendon • Oliver O'Donovan • Stanley Grenz **Socio-Critical Hermeneutics** • Liberation Theology • Feminist Theology • Black Theology

Chart 93

Diagrammatic Overview of Major Philosophies

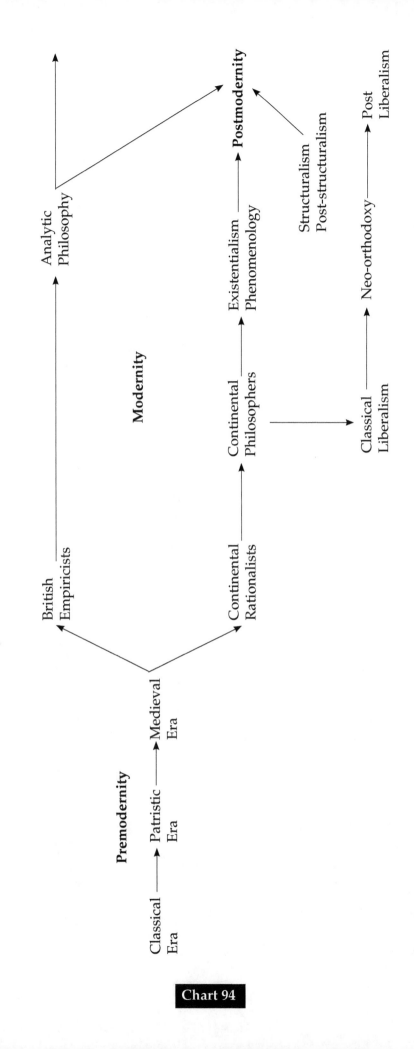

Premodernity

Classical Era → Patristic Era → Medieval Era

British Empiricists → Analytic Philosophy

Continental Rationalists → Continental Philosophers → Existentialism Phenomenology → **Postmodernity**

Modernity

Classical Liberalism → Neo-orthodoxy → Post Liberalism

Structuralism Post-structuralism → Postmodernity

Chart 94

Diagrammatic Overview of Philosophies

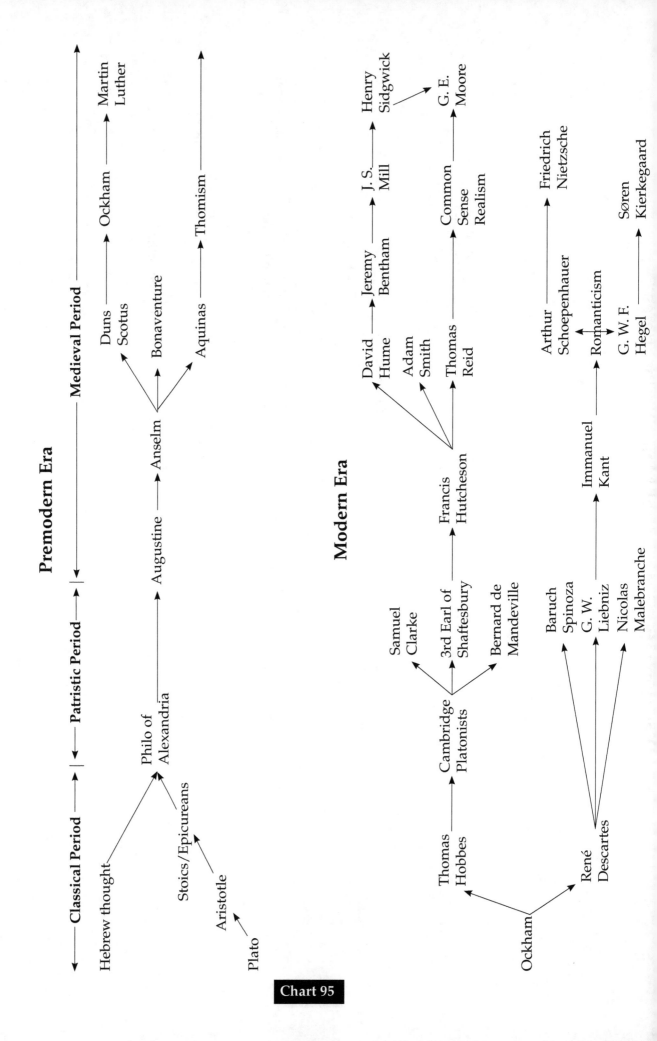

Premodern Era

Modern Era

Chart 95

Diagrammatic Overview of Philosophies (continued)

Postmodernity

Postmodernity

Analytic Philosophy

Richard Rorty
American Pragmatism

Ludwig Wittgenstein
Ordinary Language Analysis

Jacques Lacan

Post-Structuralism

Michel Foucault

Jean-Paul Sartre

Claude Lévi-Strauss

Roland Barthes

Structuralism

Martin Heidegger

Phenomenological Existentialism

Ferdinand Saussure

Edmund Husserl

Chart 95

The Premodern Era

Classical Period

	Metaethics	Moral Theory	Political Theory	Aesthetics
Plato 428/427–348/347 BC Athens, Greece	*Metaphysics of ethics* Realist, free will. *Moral epistemology* Moral knowledge is partly learned and partly innate. *Moral psychology* Welfarist.	Plato subscribed to virtue ethics. He believed that virtue is knowledge. Happiness is a person's ultimate aim, which is equated with doing well. Happiness requires certain goods, such as wealth, health, beauty, good birth and position, good fortune. 📖 *Republic, Euthyphro, Meno*	The best system of government is a polity; a tyranny is the worst. The purpose of government is to instill virtue and to maintain order. 📖 *Republic, Laws*	Beauty is functional (teleological). Beauty is transcendental. Art is imitation. Government should exercise censorship to protect the virtue of its citizens. 📖 *Phaedrus, Laws, Republic, Hippias, Symposium*
Aristotle 384/383–322 BC Athens, Greece	*Metaphysics of ethics* Realist, free will. *Moral epistemology* Moral knowledge is partly due to reason, partly innate. *Moral psychology* Welfarist, his system allowed for supererogation.	Ethics is the science of character. Persons of character are virtuous. The virtues are in accordance with the natural law. Persons of character gain happiness (*eudaimonia* and *makarios*). Prudence unifies the intellectual and moral virtues. 📖 *Nicomachean Ethics, Eudomean Ethics, Magna Moralia*	Humans are social animals. Ethics are seen as part of politics. The purpose of government is to maintain order and to develop virtue in its citizens. 📖 *Politics, Economics*	Beauty is dependent on size, proportion, fitness. Art is imitation and should be censored to ensure a virtuous society. 📖 *Poetics*

Chart 96

Classical Period (continued)

	Metaethics	Moral Theory	Political Theory
Stoics 322 BC–AD 180 Greece **Major philoso-phers:** Zeno, Cicero, Epictetus	*Metaphysics of ethics* Moral realist, determinist. *Moral epistemology* Moral knowledge is partly innate, partly through reason. *Moral psychology* Welfarist, altruist.	They subscribed to virtue ethics based on natural law. The Stoics employed many of Aristotle's ideas. They emphasized the order created by the *Logos*. They believed that we can make the right decisions through the use of reason. Emotions prevent one from thinking clearly and should be minimized. They believed that everything was predetermined. The Stoics came from the ruling class. They were few in number and emphasized the individual.	
Epicureans 322–351 BC Athens, Greece **Major philosopher:** Epicurus	*Metaphysics of ethics* Realist, libertarian free will. *Moral epistemology* Partly innate, partly reason. *Moral psychology* Hedonist, altruist.	They subscribed to virtue ethics. The good life is one acted wisely and thus avoids unnecessary trouble. The Epicureans came from the lower class, many of whom were slaves. The Epicureans emphasized the community over the individual.	
Augustine AD 354–430 Hippo, Egypt	*Metaphysics of ethics* Realist, determinist. *Moral epistemology* Moral knowledge is partly innate, partly learned. *Moral psychology* Welfarist and altruistic, but people need God's grace to live righteously. By God's grace, supererogation is possible.	Virtue ethics: The only virtuous person is the person who has Jesus Christ. The Holy Spirit creates the theological virtues in the believer. The believer can then gain the cardinal virtues. Love (*agape, caritas*) is the unifying virtue. The believer gains blessedness (*beatitudo*). Scripture is important because it orders man's loves and desires in accordance with the will of God. The lost person can gain only *eudaimonia*. Augustine comments that the virtuous pagan has only excellent vices. Augustine also dealt with the Pelagian heresy, a recurring problem. 📖 *On Free Will, On Christian Teaching, Against the Pelagians*	The church and the state coexist. There are two swords, one held by the church, the other given by the state. There are two levels of law: eternal law and temporal law. 📖 *City of God*

Chart 96

Medieval Period

	Metaethics	Moral Theory	Political Theory	Aesthetics
Bonaventure 1221–74 Tuscany, Paris, Albano, Lyons	*Metaphysics of ethics* Realist, determinist. *Moral epistemology* Moral knowledge is partly innate, partly learned. *Moral psychology* Welfarist and altruistic, but people need the grace of God to live righteously. By God's grace, supererogation is possible.	Bonaventure's system is essentially Augustinian, but it also includes ideas from Aristotle's ethics. The Holy Spirit re-creates believers with the theological virtues. Believers then gain the cardinal virtues. Believers need the Scriptures to order their affections in accordance with the will of God. 📖 *Breviloquium*	Bonaventure's system is essentially Augustinian. The civil government derives its authority from God. There are four levels of law: • eternal law • divine law • natural law • civil law Bonaventure believed that civil law should be based on natural law.	Beauty is a transcendental attribute of being. Bonaventure equated the beautiful with the true and the good. Whatever has being has form, and whatever has form has beauty. Goodness and beauty have God as their source. 📖 *Breviloquium; Itinerarium; De Reductione Artium ad Theologiam*
Thomas Aquinas 1224–74 Paris, France	*Metaphysics of ethics* Realist, free will. *Moral epistemology* Cognitivist; moral knowledge is partly innate, partly learned. *Moral psychology* Welfarist and altruistic, but people need the grace of God to live righteously. By God's grace, supererogation is possible.	Essentially Augustinian virtue ethics. Aquinas added Aristotle's philosophy to Augustine's theology. He believed that nature and grace work together. The Holy Spirit creates the theological virtues in believers, and cardinal virtues follow. 📖 *Summa Theologiae; Summa Contra Gentiles*	The state derives its authority from God. There is a hierarchy of laws: • eternal law • divine law • natural law • civil law Civil law should conform to the natural law. 📖 *On the Kingship or Governance of Rulers* (*Summa Theologiae: The Treatise on Law,* q. 90–97)	Aquinas, like Bonaventure, equated the true, the beautiful, and the good.

Chart 97

Medieval Period (continued)

John Duns Scotus 1265–1308 Scotland	*Metaphysics of ethics* Realist, based on divine command. *Moral epistemology* Cognitivist; moral knowledge is partly innate, partly through reason. *Moral psychology* Welfarist, but people need God's grace to live righteously. By God's grace, supererogation is possible.	Scotus subscribed to virtue ethics based on natural law with divine command theory. He believed that God's will is consistent with his divine nature. Thus Scotus has similarities with Aquinas and Ockham. 📖 *De Primo Principio*	Political authority depends on the agreement of the community. Legislators need legitimate authority and prudence to rule effectively. Civil law should always be in accord with natural law.
William Ockham 1290?–1349 England	*Metaphysics of ethics* Realist, based on divine command theory. *Moral epistemology* Realist, based on divine command theory. *Moral psychology* Promotionist, but people need God's grace to live righteously.	Ockham reacted against Aquinas's realism. His nominalism caused him to reject any form of Thomistic natural law. He still used the terms of natural law to mean unchangeable commands of human reason and natural equality of humans before the fall. He supported divine voluntarism and rejected human reason.	Ockham thought that natural law was the foundation of the law of nations (*ius gentium*).

Chart 97

Reformation Period

	Metaethics	Ethical Theory	Political Theory
Francisco Suárez 1548–1617 Spain, Portugal	*Metaphysics of ethics* Realist. *Moral epistemology* Internalist. *Moral psychology* Welfarist and altruistic.	Suárez combined the moderate realism of Thomistic natural law with the voluntarism of Ockham and the nominalists. The will of God is the obligatory force behind natural law. Consequently, natural law is binding on the conscience. 📖 *On Laws; God the Law Giver*	Suárez believed that natural freedom requires the consent of the governed for any political system to have legitimacy.
Hugo Grotius 1583–1645 Netherlands	*Metaphysics of ethics* Realist, free will. *Moral epistemology* Cognitivist, internalist. *Moral psychology* Promotionist and altruistic.	Grotius attempted to use natural law to resolve the problem between Protestants and Catholics. Natural law would still apply to everyone even if God does not exist. He believed that God is, in fact, the source of natural law. He rejected virtue ethics. 📖 *On the Law of War and Peace*	Grotius emphasized the implications of natural law for international law. The right to wage war results from the right to self-defense. He used natural law to defend slavery. He also emphasized individual natural rights for a just war. 📖 *On the Law of War and Peace*

Chart 98

Reformation Period (continued)

Martin Luther 1483–1546 Germany	*Metaphysics of ethics* Luther subscribed to moral realism based on divine command theory. He believed that the human will was free but bound by sin. *Moral epistemology* Cognitivist, internalist. *Moral psychology* Promotionist: people need God's grace to live righteously.	Luther was influenced by Ockham and attempted to move in a more Augustinian direction than Aquinas. He rejected Aquinas's view of nature and grace. Human reason has a place only in secular matters. In sacred matters, reason is a source of corruption. As a result, Luther rejected virtue ethics. Luther believed that grace comes upon believers before they can merit it. 📖 *The Bondage of the Will*	Luther was essentially Augustinian. People are governed by a divine ruler and an earthly one. The church should work with the state. The state derives its authority from God. Human reason is sufficient for matters of the state.
John Calvin 1509–64 Paris, Basel, Geneva	*Metaphysics of ethics* Calvin subscribed to moral realism and determinism. *Moral epistemology* Moral knowledge is partly innate and partly learned. *Moral psychology* Welfarist and altruistic.	Calvin held to divine command theory with natural law. The natural law can provide some guidance to the unregenerate, but it cannot act as a stand-in for God's grace. 📖 *Institutes of the Christian Religion*	People are social creatures who are governed by a divine ruler and an earthly one. The church works with the state. The state derives its authority from God.

Chart 98

The Modern Era

British Empiricists

	Metaethics	Ethical Theory	Political Theory	Aesthetics
Thomas Hobbes 1588–1679 England	*Metaphysics of ethics* Irrealist, free will. *Moral epistemology* Internalist. *Moral psychology* Instrumentalist, egoistic.	Hobbes's ethical theory was deontological and consequentialist. He held to social contract theory. Man in his state of nature is in a state of war. Man's life is "solitary, nasty, short and brutish." Morality is not natural; it is a human invention. Natural law means to do at all costs what one needs to do to preserve oneself. 📖 *Leviathan*	Because people are essentially evil, a strong government is needed to protect weaker people from those who are stronger. People should seek peace through a social contract. At birth people enter into a social contract that they cannot get out of. The individual has a minimum of rights, but even these are subject to the needs of the state. The sovereign may not take lives without sufficient reason. 📖 *Leviathan*	
Cambridge Platonists (*See **note** at right*)	*Metaphysics of ethics* Realist. *Moral epistemology* Externalist, moral sense. *Moral psychology* Altruistic, welfarist.	Because of Scripture, they believed that humans have a conscience, or moral sense. It was their intent to defend a Christian interpretation of reality in which to ground their views on Christian morality. 📖 *The True Intellectual System of the Universe* by Ralph Cudworth (1678)		*Note:* The Cambridge Platonists were all clergymen who were graduates of Emmanuel College, Cambridge University. They were not all Platonists, but they all emphasized Scripture.

Chart 99

	Metaethics	Ethical Theory	Political Theory	Aesthetics
John Locke 1632–1704 England	*Metaphysics of ethics* Realist, free will. *Moral epistemology* Internalist. *Moral psychology* Welfarist, altruistic.	Ethics are based on natural law. Virtues support Locke's view of religious toleration. The state of nature is one of peace, goodwill, and mutual dependence. 📖 *Essay Concerning Human Understanding; Essays on the Law of Nature*	Natural rights are based on natural law. Locke emphasized natural equality. Primary rights are the right to life, liberty, and property. People give up some of their natural rights to join in the social contract. They retain their right to rebellion. Lack of protest is tacit consent. The purpose of government is to render our freedom more secure. Government is given the power to punish. Other governmental powers should be minimized. Locke was concerned with the problems of religion (Protestant/Catholic) and the monarchy. The primary virtue is toleration. 📖 *Two Treatises on Government*	
Anthony Ashley Cooper (Third Earl of Shaftesbury) 1671–1713 England, France	*Metaphysics of ethics* Realist, free will. *Moral epistemology* Externalist, moral sense. *Moral psychology* Welfarist, altruistic.	A person's individual good consists in the harmony of his or her appetites, affections, and passions under the control of reason. Moral knowledge is gained through a moral sense. 📖 *Characteristics of Men, Manners, Opinions, Times*		The moral sense is combined with an aesthetic sense. Aesthetic knowledge is gained through this aesthetic sense. 📖 *Characteristics of Men, Manners, Opinions, Times*

Chart 99

British Empiricists (continued)

	Metaethics	Ethical Theory	Political Theory	Aesthetics
Samuel Clarke 1675–1729 England	*Metaphysics of ethics* Realist, free will. *Moral psychology* Supererogation, welfarist.	Clarke was a minister who based ethics on the nature of God. He had a high view of human reason. Clarke contended that morality works in a way that is almost mathematical. He believed that God so ordered the universe that morality can be viewed as a science. He focused on obligations that are rational and traditional. These include duties to God, to one's neighbor, and to oneself. Clarke does not seem to have considered the works of Shaftesbury, but he did contend with Leibniz.		
Bernard de Mandeville 1670–1733 England (Dutch émigré)	*Metaphysics of ethics* Realist. *Moral psychology* Supererogation, welfarist.	Mandeville rejected natural law. He believed that passion interfered with the public good. Virtue always acts for the benefit of others. Passions are dangerous; only rational ambition suffices for virtue. Without self-denial there is no virtue.		
Francis Hutcheson 1694–1759 Scotland	*Metaphysics of ethics* Realist. *Moral epistemology* Externalist. *Moral psychology* Welfarist, altruistic.	Hutcheson systematized moral sense theory and developed utilitarianism. Love is the basic factor of morality. 📖 *An Inquiry into the Origin of Our Ideas of Virtue or Moral Good; Essay on the Nature and Conduct of the Passions and Affections, with Illustrations on the Moral Sense; Philosophae Moralis Institutio Compendiaria.*	Economics: developed division of labor. Natural rights derive from natural law. 📖 *System of Moral Philosophy; Short Introduction to Moral Philosophy*	Systematized aesthetic sense (taste). There are different categories of beauty. 📖 *An Inquiry into the Origin of Our Ideas of Beauty and Virtue*

Chart 99

	Metaethics	Ethical Theory	Political Theory	Aesthetics
Joseph Butler 1692–1752 England	*Metaphysics of ethics* Realist. *Moral epistemology* Externalist, conscience. *Moral psychology* Promotionist.	Bishop Joseph Butler believed that people know right and wrong by means of a conscience. People can see that some things are natural and others unnatural. Benevolence and self-love are the two motivating factors in all people. Conscience regulates these impulses. Butler thought that human benevolence should have limits because people are also responsible for their own well-being. 📖 *Fifteen Sermons*		
David Hume 1711–76 Scotland	*Metaphysics of ethics* Irrealist. *Moral epistemology* Externalist; the passions are the moral sense. *Moral psychology* Hedonistic, instrumentalist, altruistic.	Hume was a student of Francis Hutcheson and best friend to Adam Smith. He argued, "You cannot derive ought from is" (the fact/value dichotomy), meaning that ethics has nothing to do with metaphysics. Hume used his argument against induction to remove metaphysical assumptions from ethics. Consequently, he rejected naturalism in any form. The moral sense is nothing more than the passions. Reason is and ought always to be a slave of the passions. Hume did not believe in objective moral facts. Nonetheless, he did believe that morality is useful. 📖 *An Enquiry Concerning the Principles of Morals*	Political economics. Humans are egoistic and driven by their love for gain. Hume took a largely historical approach to economics. 📖 *Writings on Economics*	Hume distinguished between beauty, perception of beauty, and judgments of beauty. Beauty commands our affections and approbation. Aesthetic judgments are based on the passions. 📖 *A Treatise of Human Nature*

Chart 99

British Empiricists (continued)

	Metaethics	Ethical Theory	Political Theory	Aesthetics
Adam Smith 1723–90 Scotland	*Metaphysics of ethics* Moral realist. *Moral epistemology* Externalist; the passions are the moral sense. *Moral psychology* Welfarist, egoist.	Humans are born with an innate capacity for sympathy. They also have an innate desire for esteem. Our care for others results in the admiration that others have for us. Smith emphasized the virtues of prudence, self-love, courage, duty, and benevolence. He deplored hatred and anger because they poison happiness. Moral duty is based on the rules of justice, chastity, and veracity. These facts affect every aspect of human life, e.g., social, political, and economic aspects of human existence. Consequently, this work provides a philosophical foundation for his *Wealth of Nations*. 📖 *The Theory of Moral Sentiments*	Many consider Smith to be the father of modern economic theory because he was primarily concerned with economic growth. Smith assumed that "men are not angels"; that is, we act in our own self-interest, not for the common good. He was concerned to create an economic system wherein there were incentives to act for the common good because it benefited oneself. Smith emphasized the efficiency of privately owned property. Private ownership is beneficial to society as a whole. 📖 *An Inquiry into the Nature and Causes of the Wealth of Nations* (better known as *The Wealth of Nations*)	

Chart 99

	Metaethics	Ethical Theory	Political Theory	Aesthetics
Jeremy Bentham 1748–1832 England	*Metaphysics of ethics* Irrealist. *Moral epistemology* Externalist, hedonist. *Moral psychology* Hedonistic instrumentalist, egoistic.	"Nature has placed man under the governance of two sovereign masters, pain and pleasure." Bentham emphasized the principle of utility, which he called "the greatest happiness principle." He was concerned with the common good. He wanted to ensure the greatest amount of good for the greatest number of those involved in any situation. For this purpose, he developed a **hedonistic calculus** (or felicific calculus) to determine the amount of pleasure and pain that would result from any action. This calculus includes such things as the amount of pleasure to be gained, the certainty of pleasure, the number of people involved in the pleasure, and the intensity of the pleasure. Bentham was an **act utilitarian.** 📖 *Introduction to the Principles of Morals and Legislation*	Bentham emphasized security, equality, and liberty. The legislator should choose the rules that best promote the general happiness. Liberty is a branch of security. Punishment is a necessary evil that can only be justified by the principle of utility. Punishment is divided into five sanctions: sympathetic, moral, religious, political, and physical. Punishment provides rights and security. Bentham believed that the legislator should be understood and controlled. 📖 *Fragment on Government*	

Chart 99

British Empiricists (continued)

	Metaethics	Ethical Theory	Political Theory	Aesthetics
John Stuart Mill 1806–73 England	*Metaphysics of ethics* Irrealist. *Moral epistemology* Moral knowledge results from pleasure and pain. *Moral psychology* Welfarist and altruistic.	Mill was a **rule utilitarian**, meaning that he believed people should follow the right set of rules that maximize utility. He believed that Bentham was right about many things; however, he thought that Bentham had a faulty view of human nature. He held that happiness resulting from morality is not about the agent's happiness but instead about the greatest amount of happiness for all concerned. He believed that happiness is not *a* good, but *the* good. Mill appealed to human nature rather than pleasure as a standard. "I regard utility as the ultimate appeal on all ethical questions, but it must be utility in the largest sense, grounded on the permanent interests of man as a progressive being." Thus he emphasized the social nature of man. 📖 *Utilitarianism*	Mill believed that the principle of utility requires government to allow individuals to develop freely. Mill emphasized the value of private liberty. Direct democracy is the best form of government. 📖 *Essays on Some Unsettled Questions of Political Economy; Principles of Political Economy; On Liberty; Considerations on Representative Government*	
Henry Sidgwick 1838–1900 England	*Metaphysics of ethics* Realist. *Moral epistemology* Intuition. *Moral psychology* Welfarist.	One cannot derive "ought" from "is." He emphasized the morality of common sense. Intuitionism led Sedgwick to universal hedonism or utilitarianism. 📖 *Methods of Ethics; Outlines of the History of Ethics for English Readers; Lectures on the Ethics of Green, Spencer and Martineau*		

Chart 99

Analytic Philosophers

	Metaethics	Ethical Theory	Aesthetics
G. E. Moore 1873–1958 England	*Metaphysics of ethics* Realist. *Moral epistemology* Intuitionism. *Moral psychology* Internalist.	Moore led the way against idealist philosophy and began the Anglo-American analytic philosophy movement. His *Principia Ethica* is the first work of metaethics in the last century. Moore was an act utilitarian who argued against any form of naturalism or metaphysical ethics. The word *good* is indefinable. Moral knowledge is gained through intuition. 📖 *Principia Ethica*	*Beauty*, like *good*, is an indefinable term. We know beauty by intuition.
A. J. Ayer 1910–89 England	*Metaphysics of ethics* Irrealist. *Moral epistemology* Moral knowledge is about emotions. *Moral psychology* Instrumentalist.	Ayer was a radical empiricist who promoted logical empiricism. Logical empiricism asserts that logical statements are based on linguistic conventions. Consequently, ethical statements are meaningless because they are not verifiable. Ethical statements only express the feelings of the speaker. This is known as *emotivism*. As such, ethical statements cannot be true or false. 📖 *Language, Truth and Logic*	
W. D. Ross 1877–1971 England	*Metaphysics of ethics* Realist. *Moral epistemology* Intuition. *Moral psychology* Welfarist.	Ross was primarily concerned with metaethics. He believed that moral knowledge is intuited. Moral principles are self-evident and cannot be reduced or unified into a general principle; they are absolute. Ross took a deontological approach to ethics known as **graded absolutism**. He emphasized seven prima facie duties: promise keeping, fidelity, gratitude, goodwill, justice, self-improvement, nonmaleficence. Ross did not believe that one can have conflicts of duties, because some are overridable. Intuition helps the moral agent resolve hypothetical conflicts. 📖 *The Right and the Good*	

Chart 100

Analytic Philosophers (continued)

	Metaethics	Ethical Theory	Aesthetics
R. M. Hare 1919–2002 England	*Metaphysics of ethics* Irrealist. *Moral epistemology* Reason. *Moral psychology* Instrumentalist.	Most of Hare's work was in metaethics. Hare rejected emotivism and intuitionism and emphasized prescriptivism. In other words, moral language is prescriptive, like a command. There are three levels of ethical thinking. The first level is metaethical and emphasizes prescriptivism and universalizability. The second or intuitive level concerns normative judgments. This level is employed when we consider ethical rules or principles. The third or critical level solves problems that the intuitive level cannot. Hare connected act utilitarianism to this critical level of ethical thought. This is known as indirect utilitarianism. Indirect utilitarianism avoids the conflicts of direct utilitarianism. 📖 *The Language of Morals; Applications of Moral Philosophy; Essays in Moral Theory; Essays in Bioethics*	
J. L. Mackie 1917–81 Australia	*Metaphysics of ethics* Irrealist, determinist. *Moral epistemology* Skeptic. *Moral psychology* Instrumentalist.	Mackie was an atheist who did not believe that moral facts exist. He did, however, believe that morality is useful. He took a rule utilitarian approach to ethics. 📖 *Ethics: Inventing Right and Wrong; Hume's Moral Theory*	
G. E. M. Anscombe 1919–2001 England	*Metaphysics of ethics* Realist. *Moral epistemology* Cognitivist. *Moral psychology* Welfarist, altruistic.	A student of Ludwig Wittgenstein. She concluded that modern moral philosophy is faulty because (1) it functions with an inadequate philosophy of psychology, (2) the concepts of moral obligation and duty are harmful, and (3) the differences of well-known British moral philosophers from Sidgwick to the present day are insignificant. She coined the term *consequentialism* to describe the dominant moral system of British philosophers. She urged a return to ancient Greek moral philosophy. 📖 *Ethics, Religion and Politics: Collected Philosophical Papers,*	

Chart 100

	Metaethics	Ethical Theory	Aesthetics
John Rawls 1921–2002 United States	*Metaphysics of ethics* Realist. *Moral epistemology* Sentiments, passions. *Moral psychology* Welfarist.	Rawls was a contractarian. He proposed a utopian form of government based on justice. Rawls equated justice with fairness. According to Rawls, "each person possesses an inviolability founded on justice that even the welfare of society as a whole cannot override. Therefore in a just society the rights secured by justice are not subject to political bargaining or to the calculus of social interests." He held two principles of justice: (1) each person involved in a society has an equal right to the most extensive liberty possible for all; (2) social and economic inequalities in a society are just only if they result in compensating benefits for all. 📖 *A Theory of Justice, Justice as Fairness*	
Martha Nussbaum 1947– United States	*Metaphysics of ethics* Realist. *Moral epistemology* Passions. *Moral psychology* Welfarist.	Nussbaum takes a feminist approach to philosophy. She believes that males have imposed a patriarchal view of reality upon the world. This view has forced women to accept certain preconceived roles. Nussbaum endorses a virtue ethic apart from natural law. Her later works emphasize the place of the emotions in moral judgment. 📖 *Upheavals of Thought*	
Philippa Foot 1920– England, United States	*Metaphysics of ethics* Realist. *Moral epistemology* *Moral psychology* Welfarist.	After studying Thomas Aquinas, Foot concluded that virtue ethics combined with natural law is the correct approach to ethics. She is noted for her opposition to both emotivism and prescriptivism. Foot is also noted for her work concerning rationality and moral action. 📖 *Theories of Ethics; Virtues and Vices, and other Essays in Moral Philosophy; Natural Goodness*	

Chart 100

Analytic Philosophers (continued)

Metaethics	Ethical Theory	Aesthetics
Alasdair MacIntyre 1929– England, United States	*Metaphysics of ethics* Realist. *Moral epistemology* Reason in virtue, prudence *Moral psychology* Welfarist, altruistic.	Perhaps the most significant moral philosopher of the last century. His *After Virtue* caused many moral philosophers to reevaluate moral theory and to seriously consider virtue ethics. MacIntyre was influenced by Anscombe, who urged a return to ancient Greek morality. MacIntyre critiques contemporary moral theory by comparing it to ancient Greek ethics. He argues that the world is ruled by managers, esthetes, and therapists. He emphasizes a return to virtue ethics but without metaphysical biology. In his latest works, MacIntyre has come to value the significance of metaphysical biology for ethics. 📖 *After Virtue; Three Rival Versions of Moral Enquiry; Dependent Rational Animals; Whose Justice, Which Rationality?*	

Chart 100

Continental Rationalists

	Metaethics	Ethical Theory	Political Theory	Aesthetics
Baruch Spinoza 1632–77 Netherlands	*Metaphysics of ethics* Realist, determinist. *Moral epistemology* Moral knowledge is gained through reason. *Moral psychology* Welfarist, altruistic.	Spinoza's approach to ethics is reminiscent of the Stoics. It is essentially premodern and teleological. His *Ethics* has five parts: God, the nature and origin of the mind, the nature and origin of the emotions, human reason, and human freedom. Spinoza was a metaphysical monist. He believed that there is only one substance, and that substance is God. God is the highest good. Seeking after God is the best thing one can do. Spinoza emphasized virtue and natural law. He believed that the fundamental emotions are desire, pleasure, and pain. All other emotions derive from these. Good is equated with pleasure, and evil is equated with pain. 📖 *Ethics*	Democracy is the most natural and the best form of government. Democracy allows for the most individual liberty. The state should allow people to live together rationally and peacefully. The state has the power to make and enforce laws. Individual citizens should obey these laws. Spinoza thought that biblical interpretation affects political regimes. The result is religious wars. He developed the historical-critical methodology to demonstrate that politics should not be influenced by theological positions (Protestant, Catholic, or Jewish). 📖 *Theological Political Treatise*	

Chart 101

Continental Rationalists (continued)

	Metaethics	Ethical Theory	Political Theory	Aesthetics
Jean Jacques Rousseau 1712–78 Switzerland, France	*Metaphysics of ethics* Irrealist, free will. *Moral epistemology* Emotivist, intuition. *Moral psychology* Instrumentalist.	Humans are essentially good. It is the artificiality of society that corrupts them. Rousseau rejects natural law and believes that reason is the key to morality. Right and wrong are determined by the emotions. Moral goodness is the identification of the individual will with the general will. "The voice of the people is the voice of God." His ethical theory is contractarian; in other words, it is deontological and consequentialist. 📖 *Emile*	Rousseau picks up from Hobbes and emphasizes the importance of a social contract. The will of the state should always prevail over the will of individuals. The general will is what determines what is just and what is unjust. The legislator should conform the laws of the state to the general will. The individual citizen should bring his or her will in line with the general will. 📖 *The Social Contract; Discourse on Political Economy*	📖 *Discourse on the Arts and Sciences*

Chart 101

	Metaethics	Ethical Theory	Political Theory	Aesthetics
Immanuel Kant 1724–1804 Prussia	*Metaphysics of ethics* Realist, free will; the good is goodwill. *Moral psychology* Cognitivist, internalist. *Moral epistemology* Promotionist.	Kant emphasized that moral knowledge results from practical reason because it is universal. He was an altruist who argued that goodwill is evident when one acts in accordance with duty. To act for any other reason invalidates the goodness of an act. He rejected any hypothetical imperatives. For these reasons, Kant emphasized the idea of autonomy of the will. Autonomy allows for a categorical imperative. Kant made a moral argument for the existence of God. He believed that virtue and happiness are not united in this life, so they must be in the next. Kant argued that there is a postmortem judgment. God will reward the good and punish the wicked in the next life. 📖 *Groundwork for a Metaphysics of Morals; Critique of Practical Reason; Metaphysics of Morals*	Kant was a contractarian, because moral truths are impartial and are shared by all. Contractarianism connects morality and mutual acceptability, meaning that all reasonable people would agree that they should act in accordance with these principles. Kant believed that the state is good in itself. He did not believe that revolution is ever warranted. He also believed that countries should form a league of nations to prevent the possibility of war. 📖 *Groundwork for a Metaphysics of Morals*	Kant took an objectivist approach to aesthetics based on an absolutist view of beauty. He argued that aesthetic judgments result from a special power. These judgments are in accordance with objective rules. Teleological judgments are universal because they are based on reason. 📖 *Critique of Judgment*

Chart 101

Continental Philosophers

	Metaethics	Ethical Theory	Political Theory	Aesthetics
G. W. F. Hegel 1770–1831 Germany	*Metaphysics of ethics* Realist. *Moral epistemology* Romanticist. *Moral psychology* Welfarist, altruistic.	Hegel employed a virtue ethics. There are three components to Hegel's ethics: 1. *Geist*—communal mind. 2. *Sittlichkeit*—communal spirit. 3. Reason—Reason has a place (however small) in decision making, along with intuition and feeling. Hegel modeled his ethical system after Aristotle. He emphasized the duties rather than the rights of the individual. He placed the community over the individual. 📖 *Philosophy of Right*	Hegel used his dialectical method to explain his political philosophy. He contrasts the state with civil society. Government is an aspect of the state. He viewed the state as a self-conscious ethical substance. Rights are established from the universal rational mind. The mature state preserves the rights and liberty of the individual. 📖 *Philosophy of Right*	Hegel's philosophy of art is based on an essence of aesthetic consciousness. Art and religion are aspects of human spirituality. The Absolute is seen in objects of sense. The Absolute is manifested in these objects of sense. The Absolute is beautiful. This idealist approach to philosophy results in aesthetic intuition.

Chart 102

	Metaethics	Ethical Theory	Political Theory	Aesthetics
Arthur Schopenhauer 1788–1860 Germany	*Metaphysics of ethics* Determinist. *Moral epistemology* Romanticist. *Moral psychology* Psychological egoism, ethical altruism.	Schopenhauer was an atheist who rejected Kant's ethics completely. He believed that all human action is based on the will to live. We have no free will, but we are still responsible for our actions. Our character is unchanging because our essence is unchanging. Our character is a unique mix of egoism, altruism, hedonism, and malice. Schopenhauer emphasized an ethic of compassion. According to Schopenhauer, death is not to be feared, but we should not commit suicide. 📖 *The World as Will and Representation*		Schopenhauer believed that the will is suspended during an aesthetic experience. Such an experience results in a state of calm, in which the will is not involved. He focused primarily on art. The true artist is a kind of genius who has a unique ability to function without the will for the period of his artistic work.

Chart 102

Continental Philosophers (continued)

	Metaethics	Ethical Theory	Political Theory	Aesthetics
Søren Kierkegaard 1813–55 Denmark	*Metaphysics of ethics* Realist. *Moral epistemology* Romanticist. *Moral psychology* Egoist.	Kierkegaard attempted to answer the question, "What should one do to find peace and significance?" Central to his philosophy is the existing individual. He wrote, "The real action is not the external act, but an internal decision in which the individual puts an end to the mere possibility and identifies himself with the content of his thought in order to exist in it." Kierkegaard specified three ways of choosing: the aesthetic, the ethical, and the religious. The aesthetic individual does not take choice seriously but lives in the moment. The ethical individual strives after moral ideals. The religious individual is willing to make a leap of faith. Christian ethics are based on God's command to love one another. 📖 *Works of Love; Concluding Unscientific Postscript*		

Chart 102

	Metaethics	Ethical Theory	Political Theory	Aesthetics
Friedrich Nietzsche 1844–1900 Germany	*Metaphysics of ethics* Irrealist, determinist. *Moral epistemology* Epistemology and ethics are replaced by hermeneutics. *Moral psychology* Amoralist.	Nietzsche was an atheist who believed that there is no objective morality. As such, right and wrong are determined by power. The weak attempt to control the strong by forcing their values on them. This is a will to power. The superman is the individual who is unrestrained in his use of his will to power. He is unaffected by the petty moralistic acid of the weak. The superman cares only for himself and his children. 📖 *Beyond Good and Evil; Thus Spoke Zarathustra; Ecce Homo; Genealogy of Morals*	Nietzsche endorsed a master/slave morality. The best kind of government is one in which a small but immoral ruling class is in charge of a large but moral slave class.	Just as there is no objective truth or morality, there is no objective beauty. Once again, there are no facts, only interpretations. Beauty is determined by power.

Chart 102

Continental Philosophers (continued)

	Metaethics	Ethical Theory	Political Theory	Aesthetics
Martin Heidegger 1889–1976 Germany	*Metaphysics of ethics* Irrealist, free will. *Moral epistemology* Reason, what is right for the individual. *Moral psychology* Instrumentalist.	Heidegger considered morality a secondary issue because being has to come first. Individuals must do what is right for them because they are thrown into an alien and hostile world without any choice in the matter. Being contains a decisionist aspect that requires persons to explore the possibilities available to them and to take decisive action. This does not mean that Heidegger glorified barbaric brutality or a denial of values. Heidegger did not completely reject theism and connected being with religion. 📖 *Being and Time*		

Chart 102

	Metaethics	Ethical Theory	Political Theory	Aesthetics
Jean-Paul Sartre 1905–80 France	*Metaphysics of ethics* Irrealist, free will. *Moral epistemology* Reason, what is right for the individual. *Moral psychology* Instrumentalist.	Sartre believed that existence has a moral value. He said that there is no way to separate morality from our actions. Every individual is unique, so one cannot base ethics on human nature. Sartre emphasized free will and choice. He also emphasized the subjectivity of ethics. According to Sartre, the mind is in command of the body and the emotions. He equated emotions with actions that we choose to adopt. Consequently, one should take responsibility for one's own life and situations. To fail to do so is to act in bad faith. One has an obligation to be true to oneself. Bad faith is exemplified by inauthenticity. 📖 *Being and Nothingness*		

Chart 102

Theological Liberalism

	Metaethics	Ethical Theory
Liberalism • Friedrich Schleiermacher • Albrecht Ritschl • Adolf Harnack • Ernst Troelsch • Wilhelm Herrmann Nineteenth century Europe	*Metaphysics of ethics* Realist. *No one theory* *Moral psychology* Welfarist.	The classical liberals emphasized natural theology and deemphasized Scripture. They combined Romanticism and the historical-critical methodology with Christianity. Consequently, they downplayed the importance of doctrine. The classical liberals held the belief that no part of the New Testament was written before the second or third century AD. As a result, nothing can be known about the historical Jesus. The classical liberals asserted that Christianity was ultimately about feelings and ethics.
The Social Gospel • Walter Rauschenbusch • Washington Gladden Nineteenth century United States	*Metaphysics of ethics* Realist. *No clear theory* *Moral psychology* Welfarist, altruistic.	Rauschenbusch was a Baptist minister who studied with Albrecht Ritschl. He wanted to integrate the kingdom of God with American culture and industry. Rauschenbusch argued that there was such a disparity between the rich and the poor that there could not be justice in the land. He called on people to replace the existing economic and social structures to usher in the kingdom of God. 📖 *The Kingdom of God in America; Christianity and the Social Crisis; Christianizing the Social Order; A Theology of the Social Gospel*

Chart 103

Neo-orthodox Thinkers

	Metaethics	Ethical Theory
Karl Barth 1886–1968 Germany, Switzerland	*Metaphysics of ethics* Free will. *Moral epistemology* Conscience involves listening to God's voice. *Moral psychology* Promotionist.	Barth rejected philosophical approaches to ethics. Consequently, he rejected general revelation and natural law. Instead, Barth emphasized the Christian existing in grace. Grace gives the Christian the freedom to be what God has called him or her to be. For Barth, Christian ethics revolves around creation, reconciliation, and redemption. He believed the goodness of human conduct to be found only in God's commands. Barth equated God's election with his divine command. 📖 *Ethics; Church Dogmatics*
Dietrich Bonhoeffer 1906–45 Germany	*Metaphysics of ethics* Free will. *Moral epistemology* Internalist. *Moral psychology* Welfarist, altruistic.	Bonhoeffer believed that the individual person, his sin, God's revelation, and reconciliation in Christ can only be understood in the light of the church's sociality. He emphasized God's grace in Jesus Christ. "Grace is costly because it calls us to follow, and it is grace because it calls us to follow Jesus Christ." Because this grace cost Jesus Christ his life, it is costly. This grace is not cheap, and it calls Christ's followers to obedience. While one should not seek to suffer needlessly, still one should divest oneself of the attachments to this world. He emphasized that believers deny themselves, pick up their crosses, and follow after Christ. Jesus' command to love one another should be taken literally and unconditionally. 📖 *Ethics; The Cost of Discipleship; Sanctorum Communio; Act and Being*
Emil Brunner 1889–1966 Germany	*Metaphysics of ethics* Realist, free will. *Moral epistemology* Cognitivist. *Moral psychology* Promotionist, altruistic.	Brunner focused on anthropological theology. He thought that all social, political, and cultural beliefs presuppose an anthropology. Brunner believed that Barth made a mistake by discarding natural law and general revelation, because this left no room for common grace. He thought that there is a genuine Christian natural theology. He also emphasized the biblical idea that humans are created in the image of God. 📖 *The Divine Imperative; Justice and the Social Order; Christianity and Civilization*

Chart 104

Neo-orthodox Thinkers (continued)

	Metaethics	Ethical Theory
Rudolf Bultmann 1884–1976 Germany	*Metaphysics of ethics* Realist. *Moral psychology* Promotionist, altruistic.	Bultmann rejected the idea of any system of Christian ethics. The Christian has no special insight into the good that is unavailable to the pagan. Bultmann held these positions because he believed that ethics is an attempt by people to establish their own righteousness through works. Instead, Bultmann emphasized an existential but theocentric theology. Salvation comes in response to the gospel and causes believers to surrender all self-reliance and all attempts at self-righteousness. Instead, faith causes believers to act in radical obedience. *Christ, the End of the Law; Jesus and the Word*
Reinhold Niebuhr 1892–1971 United States	*Metaphysics of ethics* Realist. *Moral epistemology* Cognitivist. *Moral psychology* Promotionist, altruistic.	Reinhold Niebuhr emphasized original sin and realism about power politics. The individual person is capable of being a moral creature, and it is in large groups or institutions that people become immoral. He contrasted law and justice because they are two important forces that guide human action. One needs both of these in order to be truly ethical. Christianity allows one to have a proper balance of these forces. Niebuhr understood sin as pride and self-centeredness. To make matters worse, sin is universal and thus impacts everyone at every level of life. He argued that democracy is necessary and that the church cannot take a completely pacifist position. *Moral Man, Immoral Society; The Nature and Destiny of Man*
H. Richard Niebuhr 1894–1962 United States	*Metaphysics of ethics* Realist. *Moral epistemology* Cognitivist. *Moral psychology* Promotionist, altruistic.	H. Richard Niebuhr focused on the relationship between the church and culture. He listed five different types of relationship between the two: (1) Christ against culture—stresses the antagonism between the church and a fallen world; (2) Christ of culture—Christian ethics expresses the values of the world at large; (3) Christ above culture—expresses the difference between ethics based on general revelation and ethics based on the special revelation exemplified in Jesus Christ; (4) Christ and culture in paradox—even further emphasizes the difference between a fallen world and the purity of the gospel; (5) Christ the transformer of culture—culture should be transformed by the power of Christ. The church should teach and evangelize in accordance with Christian doctrine. *Christ and Culture; Radical Monotheism and Western Culture*

Chart 104

Postmodern Era

Contemporary Christian Ethicists

	Metaethics	Ethical Theory
Joseph Fletcher 1905–91 United States	*Metaphysics of ethics* Realist. *Moral epistemology* Intuition. *Moral psychology* Promotionist, altruistic.	Fletcher believed that moral knowledge can be gained only through intuition. He emphasized the use of love as a key to right action. Fletcher argued that the most loving thing in any context is the key to right action. According to Fletcher, only love is always good, and thus it should be our norm. He also equated love with justice. Fletcher did not want anyone to confuse love with liking. 📖 *Situation Ethics*
Paul Ramsey 1913–88 United States	*Metaphysics of ethics* Realist. *Moral epistemology* Cognitivist. *Moral psychology* Promotionist, altruistic.	Ramsey was critical of situation ethics. At the same time, his system also emphasized the importance of love for Christian ethics. His ethics was influenced by the moral philosophy of John Rawls. Ramsey combined love with a number of ethical principles. He distinguished between "act agapism" and "rule agapism." Act agapism is concerned with acts motivated by Christian love. Rule agapism is concerned with rules that embody love. Both act and rule agapism can embody love, and they both can be problematic. He believed that one needs to evaluate carefully the consequences of going against moral rules. 📖 *Basic Christian Ethics*
John Howard Yoder 1927–97 United States	*Metaphysics of ethics* Realist. *Moral epistemology* Cognitivist. *Moral psychology* Promotionist, altruistic.	Yoder's works reflect his Mennonite background and the influence of Karl Barth. He was a pacifist who emphasized the idea that Jesus was politically relevant. Because of his relevance, Jesus was crucified. Yoder explained the relationship of the fall to the angelic powers that are attached to creation. The human institutions of the state and marriage were established by God and reflect the sin inherent in the fall. Yoder believed that we should not revolt against these orders of creation. We should instead respond with the love of Christ. Sin cannot be defeated with sin but only with submission and obedience. 📖 *The Politics of Jesus; Preface to Theology*

Chart 105

Ethical Theory

	Metaethics	Ethical Theory
James Gustafson 1925–Present United States	*Metaphysics of ethics* Realist. *Moral epistemology* Cognitivist. *Moral psychology* Promotionist, altruistic.	Gustafson is influenced by Karl Barth, but he is also influenced by Reformed theology, Thomas Aquinas, and many others. As such, his approach to ethics is complicated but significant. Gustafson believes that there is a distinctive Christian moral character. He also believes that liberation theology is an important idea in Christian ethics. He decries sectarianism and argues that we should be motivated by our desire to serve the body of Christ. 📖 *Ethics from a Theocentric Perspective; Christ and the Moral Life; Protestant and Roman Catholic Ethics; Treasure in Earthen Vessels: The Church as a Human Community*
Stanley Hauerwas 1940–Present United States	*Metaphysics of ethics* Realist, free will. *Moral epistemology* Cognitivist. *Moral psychology* Welfarist, altruistic.	Hauerwas is a postliberal theologian who endorses virtue ethics. He does so because of the postmodern emphasis on narrative and community embraced by postliberalism. His recent works allow some place for natural law. Hauerwas emphasizes becoming the right kind of person. He also emphasizes the importance of the narrative parts of Scripture for spiritual growth. 📖 *Character and the Christian Life; After Christendom; Resident Aliens; Truthfulness and Tragedy; Vision and Virtue; Unleashing the Scripture; A Community of Character; Against the Grain of the Universe*
James McClendon 1924–2000 United States	*Metaphysics of ethics* Realist. *Moral epistemology* Cognitivist. *Moral psychology* Welfarist, altruistic.	Like Hauerwas, McClendon came from an Anabaptist tradition. As such, he emphasizes community, narrative, and virtue ethics. He argues that ethics rather than doctrine is the best place to begin the study of systematic theology. McClendon emphasizes narrative theology as opposed to the traditional propositional approach to theology. 📖 *Biography as Theology; Systematic Theology: Ethics*
Oliver O'Donovan 1945–Present England	*Metaphysics of ethics* Realist. *Moral epistemology* Cognitivist. *Moral psychology* Welfarist, altruistic.	O'Donovan approaches ethics from an evangelical perspective. He emphasizes the importance of doctrine, Scripture, and general revelation. Salvation in Jesus Christ is the starting point for Christian ethics. O'Donovan affirms the importance of the created order for Christian ethics. Salvation and redemption are eschatological, and so is Christian ethics. He asserts that the Spirit of God works in the lives of believers to guide them in all they do. It is love that moves believers to act in accordance with the created order. 📖 *Resurrection and the Moral Order; From Irenaeus to Grotius; The New Dictionary of Christian Ethics and Pastoral Theology; The Desire of the Nations; Common Objects of Love*

Chart 105

Socio-Critical Approaches to Ethics

	Metaethics	Ethical Theory
Liberation Theology **Gustavo Gutierez** 1928–Present Peru	*Metaphysics of ethics* Irrealist. *Moral epistemology* Noncognitivist. *Moral psychology* Promotionist, altruistic.	Liberation theology is a postmodern approach to theology. It is concerned with the struggle of the poor as they seek to gain justice. It argues that the rich and the powerful take advantage of the poor. Liberation theologians argue that there should be a redistribution of resources to satisfy the needs of the poor. Liberation theology is not only an ethic, but is a hermeneutic as well. It is an example of a neo-Nietzschean will to power. What is good is good for the poor. Bad or evil is whatever might be bad for the poor.
Feminist Theology **Rosemary Radforth Ruether** 1936–Present **Phyllis Trible** 1932–Present United States	*Metaphysics of ethics* Irrealist. *Moral epistemology* Noncognitivist. *Moral psychology* Promotionist, altruistic.	Feminist theology is another example of a postmodern neo-Nietzschean will to power. It is both an ethic and a hermeneutic. What is good is whatever is good for women. Bad or evil is whatever is bad for women.

Chart 106

www.ingramcontent.com/pod-product-compliance
Lightning Source LLC
LaVergne TN
LVHW060834240225
804065LV00001B/1